GREAT POTENTIAL

LATINOS

IN A CHANGING AMERICA

STEVE MOYA

authorHOUSE®

AuthorHouse™
1663 Liberty Drive
Bloomington, IN 47403
www.authorhouse.com
Phone: 1-800-839-8640

Published by AuthorHouse 5/31/2013

ISBN: 978-1-4817-3263-5 (sc)
ISBN: 978-1-4817-3264-2 (e)

Library of Congress Control Number: 2013905941

Table of Contents

Introduction

Latino Timing and the Nation's Experience

Lemuel Moya was born in the New Mexico Territory in the early 1900s. In 1924, he moved to Los Angeles where he joined the Santa Fe Railroad and became a boilermaker. Tragically, he died young, leaving behind a wife and son. They struggled to survive on her seamstress wages and the boy's newspaper sales along with some help from extended family. After high school the son joined the navy and later studied at a community college, receiving an associate of arts degree which led to an entry-level white-collar job as a purchasing agent. His fifty-year marriage produced three children who all went on to achieve success in their respective careers as a corporate executive, CPA, and office manager.

Achieving this kind of multi-generational success was not easy. It never is. Consider the story of Lemuel Moya's son who faced discrimination and even violence in 1940s Los Angeles. In 1943, as World War II was escalating, the Zoot Suit Riots between young white servicemen and Mexican Americans took place in LA, spurred on in part by soldier resentment over the fact that the stylishly dressed young Latino men were not in uniform and heading to war. Of course, Mexican Americans were well represented and performed well in all branches of the military. When the war ended, returning soldiers once again fought with Mexican Americans, particularly in East Los Angeles, so, for some, the euphoria that came with the end of war was short-lived. Meanwhile, about ninety miles north of Los Angeles, the daughter-in-law Lemuel Moya never knew faced her own struggles as a student at a segregated school in the Ventura, California area in the mid-1940s.

While this family faced many obstacles, it is even more difficult today for Latino families to duplicate the Moya's sort of success. The ascent of Lemuel's family entailed skill and hard work, but that has always been the case for those at the bottom or middle tier of society striving to move up. What he and his descendants had in their favor was *timing*—not the only factor in their success, but a critical one. The Moya family and others like them entered the country at a point in US history when a strong back and a good work ethic, despite a lack of education, could advance a family over time.

Still, the Moya's ascent into the middle class was not an easy path—a fact that holds true for most immigrants. They were making steady progress until the Great Depression hit, which presented challenges for all Americans. Members of the Moya family actually benefited from the work programs established under the New Deal, but then World War II brought tragedy and sacrifice for everyone at home, including the Moyas, whose military members mostly served in the Pacific theater.

Following the war there was a new era of prosperity in the United States; suddenly, the American Dream was within reach for millions who previously had been left out of the middle class. During this period almost every aspect of American society offered opportunity and a road to prosperity, although there were no guarantees, and the Moyas had to take advantage of almost every opportunity afforded them. The evidence is abundant that the middle class, including Latinos, flourished due to increased opportunities in several areas:

Jobs and employment: Unemployment was low in almost all parts of the country. There was a broad range of available jobs, especially in the blue-collar sectors, with good health and retirement benefits. As long as individuals were willing to look for them, there were opportunities to be found, and most people became homeowners.

Education: Access to higher education was never more plentiful as colleges and universities expanded and financing was offered through the G. I. Bill. In addition, modestly priced student loans were available for those who did not serve in the military.

Housing: The construction industry flourished, providing jobs for blue-collar workers. Millions of home buyers benefited as they took advantage of attractive financing and an abundance of modest, affordable homes in new suburban neighborhoods.

Race relations: Although the transition was not easy, desegregation eventually took hold throughout the country, resulting in substantially better minority access to employment and higher education.

The American family: One notable societal difference between the post-war era and today is that back then two incomes were not necessary to sustain families: one parent was in the workforce while the other devoted time to the family. Stay-at-home moms were the norm.

Timing: One often overlooked fact is that during this era of unbridled growth and opportunity, the Hispanic population in the United States was very small, comprising only 4.5% percent of the nation's population in 1970, growing to 22 million in 1990 and 52 million today. According to the Census there will be an estimated 95 million Hispanics in the United States by 2050.

It is important to note, therefore, that the majority of today's Latino population did not benefit from those foundational years between 1947 and 1973, an era when many (though not all) American families were able to establish an educational and socioeconomic framework which allowed them to compete in what would become a dramatically changing and highly competitive world. Today, in fact, an explosion of research confirms that socioeconomic mobility in the United States has started to deteriorate. And therein lies Latino's collective challenge: How the nation's youngest and fastest-growing population, a demographic with serious educational and economic deficiencies, dramatically alter its competitive trajectory in order to contribute to a challenged and aging America over the course of a single generation.

Old ideas about how to advance as a community will not get Latinos where they need to be and thinking of the Latino community as if it is separate from the larger society is simply wrong. Latinos comprise a unique community with its own history, culture, and language, but as it organizes, the community, and individuals, must always consider the broader societal context. This requires a deeper understanding of where American society is going, how the American economy is changing, and what new challenges America is facing. Latinos must also understand what kind of thinking drives America, how America fits within a shrinking world, and ultimately how an aging America will evolve.

This book embraces and blends the best ideas and theories from business, government, and individuals as well as the nonprofit sector, including a range of Latino experts. The overarching idea is to promote, through new thinking, a course of action which is viable, powerful, and lasting. Though the scope of my plan is national, the energy driving it will come from neighborhoods and, above all, households.

My intent is first, to briefly summarize where the majority of the Latino population stands today; second, to place this understanding within the context of the challenges and opportunities in the broader American society and the world; third, to describe the thinking that drives success in today's economy; and fourth and most important, to propose strategies and tactics to advance Latino neighborhoods and families.

Ultimately, I hope this book will advance a movement in some form because it offers fresh insights on the Latino situation, a strategic framework for dealing with it, and a set of new ideas and a solid platform which can be customized and improved upon by neighborhoods and communities.

We will see in future chapters that the challenges to dramatic Latino progress continue to be daunting, just as they were decades ago. But the opportunities are immense, too, if everyone rises to the challenge.

Hispanic America Today

Statistical Portrait of Hispanics in the United States, 2010

Population Change, by Race and Ethnicity: 2000 and 2010

Universe: 2000 and 2010 resident population

	2010 Population	2000 Population	Change 2000-2010	Percent change, 2000-2010	Share of total changes (%)
Hispanic	50,729,570	35,204,480	15,525,090	44.1	55.6
Native Born	31,912,465	21,072,230	10,840,235	51.4	38.8
Foreign born	18,817,105	14,132,250	4,684,855	33.2	16.8
White alone, not Hispanic	196,931,448	194,527,123	2,404,325	1.2	8.6
Black alone, not Hispanic	37,936,978	33,706,554	4,230,424	12.6	15.1
Asian alone, not Hispanic	14,558,242	10,088,521	4,469,721	44.3	16.0
Other, not Hispanic	9,193,451	7,895,228	1,298,223	16.4	4.6
Total	309,349,689	281,421,906	27,927,783	9.9	100.0

Note: "Other, not Hispanic" includes persons reporting single races not listed separately and persons reporting more than one race.

Source: Pew Hispanic Center tabulations of 2000 Census (5% IPUMS) and 2010 American Community Survey (1% IPUMS)

The Hispanic Population accounted for 55.6% of the total population growth of the United States from 2000 to 2010.

Then There's the New Latino Timing

Americans are victims of nostalgia if they believe that, as a nation, the United States has always been a peaceful and cooperative society. From the Civil War to Prohibition to the civil rights era and Vietnam, and all the conflicts in between, Americans have differed in their views of how the world, or at least their part of it, should function. That said, today's America appears particularly contentious.

The two major political parties seem unable even to sit at the same table in a civilized manner. Those elected to Congress have, through such behavior, driven their disapproval ratings to all-time lows. The upstart Tea Party seems to have either vocal supporters or vocal critics, with few people in the middle. Support for President Obama and his policies is fragmented at best.

Add to that political mix a new issue that has not seen the same prominence (or division) since the Great Depression. The general term is *inequality*, but it has been labeled in many different ways, including "rich versus poor," "class warfare," and "the 1 percent versus the 99 percent." This is not just media hype. According to a recent report by the Pew Research Center, the number of Americans who believe there are "strong conflicts" between the rich and the poor in the United States has risen to two-thirds—the highest number since 1992. This is just one of many high-profile societal conflicts to gain in prominence as Americans have adopted wildly diverging views on issues like immigration, religion, gay rights, the role of government, global warming and other environmental challenges, the size and role of the military, and many, many more.

Not to discount the important role of debate in a democracy, but today's constant rancor often clouds thoughtful discussion of Americans' collective future and makes it almost impossible to focus on the critical issue of the economy in an increasingly competitive world. While I still see a bright future for the nation, I question whether American families and workers can keep up in the new global economy and whether the country can create enough high-quality jobs to overcome what appears to be serious wage deflation.

Future chapters will highlight in greater detail the new economic dynamics, particularly as they apply to jobs, work skills, and competitiveness, but for now, suffice it to say that the likely American economic scenario ahead is concerning. Though the problems are complex, the critical issues revolve around demographics, incomes, and education and skills.

A main contention of this book is that if more Americans understood the very real global challenge to their economic future, they would value an investment in every American, if for no other reason than for the purposes of self-interest. They would also understand that societal cooperation is essential to effective policy making and government action, a point clearly laid out in "Reshaping the Social Contract: Demographic Distance and Our Fiscal Future," by Manual Pastor, professor of American studies and ethnicity and director of the Program for Environmental and Regional Equity (PERE) at the University of Southern California, and Vanessa Carter, data analyst at PERE. In this thoughtful article, the authors observe that two days of reckoning have come closer: the moment at which the US becomes a "majority-minority" nation (around 2042, according to census projections) and the moment at which tax and fiscal decisions are aligned with the realities of America's future.

Projected Growth

Table 1 U.S. Population, Actual and Projected 2005 and 2050

	2005	2050
Population (in millions)	296	438
Share of total		
Foreign born	12%	19%
Racial/Ethnic Groups		
White	67%	47%
Hispanic	14%	29%
Black	13%	13%
Asian	5%	9%
Age Groups		
Children (17 and younger)	25%	23%
Working age (18-64)	63%	58%
Elderly (65 and older)	12%	19%

Note: All races modified and not Hispanic: American Indian/ Alaska Native not shown. See "Methodology."

Source: Pew Research Center, 2008

Figure 1 U.S. Population, Actual and Projected: 1960-2050 (in millions)

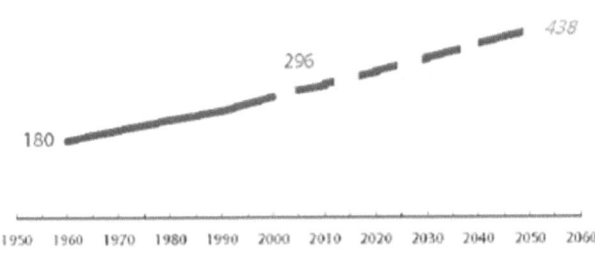

Note: Projections for 2005-2050 indicated by broken line.

Source: Pew Research Center, 2008

This trend will continue according to the US Census Bureau, which estimates that the Hispanic population in the United States will reach 95.5 million by 2050.

While it is important to consider the growth rate of America's various racial/ethnic groups, what is more important is the difference between their median ages. For non-Hispanic whites the median age is forty-two; for Asian Pacific Islanders, it is thirty-five; for African Americans it is thirty-two; and for Latinos it is twenty-seven. These differences serve to widen the racial generation gap.

This demographic reality is already obvious: nearly half (46.5 percent) of Americans under age eighteen are children of color. While it is essential that these young people become as productive as possible to spur national economic vitality, it is clear that the states with the greatest racial generation gap have less state-level capital outlays per capita and less education spending per student. At the same time, the benefits for older people, such as Social Security and Medicare, are shielded by strong political lobbies, and baby boomers have successfully resisted any tax increases while in their prime earning years. It is as if the ladder of opportunity is being pulled up just as a new generation, disproportionately of color, is entering the labor market and coming to social and political influence. This might seem economically viable in the short run, but it cannot last.

This growth dynamic has dramatic implications in the United States and around the world as populations age and birth rates drop. The US Census Bureau estimates that the number of American workers aged fifteen to sixty-four will **grow** 42 percent between 2000 and 2050, while the equivalent demographic in China will **shrink** by 10 percent, in Europe by 25 percent, in Korea by 30 percent, and in Japan by 44 percent. These are critical numbers. Paul Ashwort of the forecasting firm Capital Economics has observed that over the long term two things drive economic growth: more workers and more productivity from those workers.

It makes sense to increase opportunities for all Americans, particularly the young. This becomes an even more important issue as the United States continues to struggle with chronic unemployment: both the share of the American population that is working and the number of unemployed Americans actively looking for work are near thirty-year lows. On the other hand, targeting areas like math and science proficiency and raising those levels to those of nations like Korea or even Canada would eventually increase annual GDP growth rates by 30 to 50 percent, according to a report by Eric Hanushek of the Hoover Institution and Ludger Woessmann of the University of Munich.

Fortunately, we are beginning to understand more clearly where we are and, to some degree, where we are headed. The following chapter offers a glimpse of how Latinos got to this point.

The Youth of Hispanic America

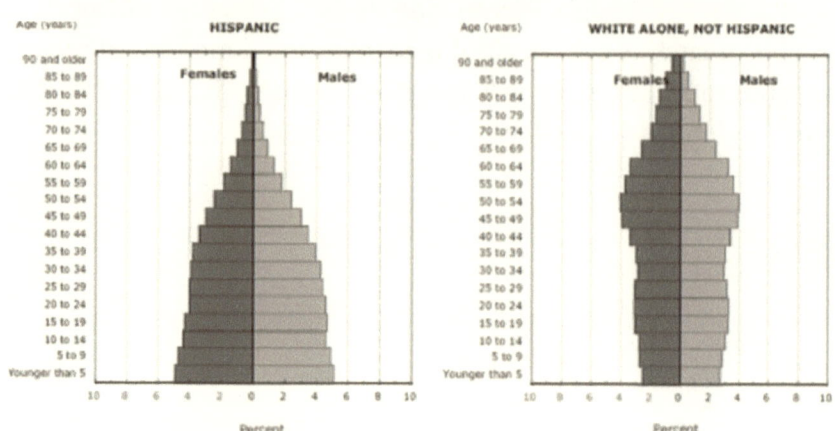

Table 9 Statistical Portrait of Hispanics in the United States, 2010

Median Age in Years, by Sex, Race and Ethnicity: 2010

Universe: 2010 resident population

	All	Male	Female
Hispanic	27	26	27
Native born	18	17	18
Foreign born	38	37	39
White alone, not Hispanic	42	40	43
Black alone, not Hispanic	32	30	34
Asian alone, not Hispanic	35	34	36
Other, not Hispanic	23	22	24
All	37	35	38

Note: "Other, not Hispanic" includes persons reporting single races not listed seperately and persons reporting more than one race

Source: Pew Hispanic Center tabulations of 2010 American Community Survey (1% IPUMS)

In 2010, the median age of the Hispanic population in America was 27, while the White alone population had a median of 42.

Latinos in the Seventies and Eighties

To many economists, 1973 marked the beginning of a gradual but steady shift in the global economy—so pervasive a shift that it would change the future for billions of people all over the world, but most notably those in the United States. Whether it is called the "knowledge" or the "information" economy there is hard evidence that a substantial realignment of the global economy was beginning, with long-term ramifications.

In many ways, the shift to the new economy was a slow build— insidious in some ways but powerful nonetheless. Most dramatically, the new economic paradigm promoted knowledge as the dominant asset to produce economic benefit. Clearly, knowledge has always been valued, but its use and value intensified as manufacturing declined and the service industry flourished. Simultaneously, knowledge-based assets helped fuel globalization as networking and connectivity became the norm.

Over time it became clear that many American workers were not prepared for this shift. While some had the educational and social background to catch up, many did not and were unqualified for the new, knowledge-based jobs in software, information processing, health care, and management. Those who entered the country as immigrants with only rudimentary schooling were marginalized from the beginning, even if they did not realize it. While their lives may have improved compared to their lives in their native countries, they faced a unique and extremely difficult challenge: to progress, and quickly, with little foundation in the new information age.

During this period, America was going through many changes, and Hispanics were part of the changing world. In October 1978, the cover of TIME magazine proclaimed that Hispanic Americans would soon be the country's largest minority. The cover story described in glowing terms how Hispanics, "now the fastest growing minority …are bidding to become an increasingly influential one." To be fair, TIME did point out that this emerging group had its share of issues, including deficiencies in language, education, and income, but hardly anyone seemed to take note of them because the era was a time of change in every part of society and this population growth was simply another manifestation of the shifts taking place in areas of social life from women's rights, to drug use, to the "new" family. Hispanics themselves were trying to understand the changes in their own communities. This immigration, which accelerated in the 1980s, combined with the Chicano Movement and other social changes, left many people in barrios throughout the nation in a state of bewilderment.

The Assimilation and Acculturation Questions

Some observers have questioned Hispanic assimilation and acculturation rates, but their analysis has often been flawed. In some cases they overly romanticize the experience of earlier immigrants which was not as smooth as some remember. More importantly, they often fail to recognize the differences between immigrant populations in the late nineteenth and early twentieth centuries and Hispanic immigrants of the last forty years as well as the different realities of these times—particularly the economic realities described earlier. Finally, too many people disregard geographic proximity and the fact that many Mexicans, for decades, were comfortable moving back and forth across the border for work for extended periods and had little reason to assimilate because they left their families in Mexico and returned to them for short periods of time.

The bottom-line is that, for the most part, Hispanic acculturation and assimilation has followed similar patterns of other populations. Ironically, while Hispanics have all along followed mainstream ideas about success, that attitude has sometimes turned into an impediment because the American Dream and the road to it have changed. Here are just a few examples of how Hispanics have bought into the mainstream frame of mind:

- They have adopted the consumer mindset and all the traps that come along with it, including debt and failure to save for the future.
- They have bought into the idea that home ownership is vital to the American Dream, even when it does not make financial sense and requires allocating too many family resources to make a monthly house payment.
- Although extended family is still important to Hispanics, there are many signs that the individualism that permeates American culture is also creeping into Hispanic communities, with a resulting lack of support from relatives when it is needed the most.
- Even though the old guarantee that "our children will do better than us" has been battered for more than a decade, it has permeated the thinking of Hispanic families

The bottom line? Chasing the "old" mainstream is a losing proposition. All Americans have to recognize that challenges have changed. The rules are different, and the goals have either evaporated or morphed. Everyone needs to run a new race in order to win in the new world.

How People Have Fared Since the Early 1970s

So what has the global economic realignment meant to the US population and the American people? It depends on who you ask. For those in finance, scientific and technical fields, and high-end services, the last thirty-plus years have been very good. Analysts point out that since the early 1990s, the jobs that have grown the most have been in either the top 20 percent or the bottom 20 percent of jobs in terms of median wages. It is essentially an hourglass distribution.

Many argue that this dynamic has contributed to an income disparity even greater than that of the 1920s. While some economists argue that the income gap has increased primarily due to the rapid pace of technological change, advocates for the working class have suggested that government policies have also played a significant role, such as anti-union actions and a failure to adequately raise the minimum wage. There seems to be general agreement that wages for the middle and bottom rungs of society have lost momentum, even if everyone does not agree on why. In fact, when adjusted for inflation, those wages have stagnated since the early seventies.

This is the point in the discussion when the "quality of life" theme appears—when conservative observers inevitably point out that almost every American household sports a big-screen television, air conditioning, and other household conveniences as well as a car or two. While this may be true, the debt that many families incur in order to have those things is a high price to pay, literally and figuratively. More importantly, the wage squeeze makes other more critical things more difficult to pay for, such as health care, education, and retirement costs.

Ultimately, wealth may tell a greater story than income—and this where the top 1 to 20 percent of Americans, those at society's apex, are even further removed from the rest of society. It is estimated that in 2007, the top 20 percent of Americans controlled 61.4 percent of the income and 93 percent of the wealth, while the top 1 percent alone controlled 42.1 percent of the wealth.

In the final analysis, it is clear that there always have been and always will be winners and losers in American society as economic adjustments continue to play out, impacting everyone. Middle-class Hispanics will compete with a broader American middle class facing the same issues; some analysts even predict that middle-class Americans will be affected by the global rise of middle-class populations who will drive up the price for basic goods as they strain inventory levels. It is safe to say that the challenges for the middle class overall will intensify.

Latinos are clearly linked to the broader American society and need to recognize and understand that dynamic. With that in mind, I would like to offer my own insights into the challenges all Americans are dealing with.

The New Challenges Facing Latinos and All Americans

Regardless of the era, there is never a dearth of challenges, and the current era is certainly no different. Among a long list of challenges Americans face, five areas stand out: growing income inequality; the widening gap in wealth between whites and minorities; the rise in American pessimism and alienation, especially among minority populations; the socioeconomic decline of men; and college as a cause for both optimism and pessimism.

The wealth gap. Rather than highlighting the numbers—that is, the overall wealth of the top 1, 5, or 10 percent—I think it is important to put such numbers in context and to illuminate some of the factors that have led to growing economic inequality, especially impacting Latinos, minorities, and less-educated Americans. In *The Great Divergence: America's Growing Inequality Crisis and What We Can Do About It*, Timothy Noah offers a broad sampling of reasons for the wealth gap, including the American education system's inability to keep up with new job demands; the introduction of more unskilled than skilled immigrants; overseas competition; the erosion of minimum wage compared to inflation; the decline of unions, particularly in the private sector; and anti-worker/anti-poor attitudes displayed by many politicians. Noah describes the growing wealth inequality as a global phenomenon, and even a casual analysis of any other country, from Mexico to China, would support that assertion.

The white-minority wealth gap. According to a Pew study, Hispanics and blacks have historically accumulated far less wealth than whites. In 2009, the median net worth was $134,992 for whites, compared with $18,359 for Hispanics. The economic decline since the Great Recession has hurt all populations, but for Hispanics the figures are most dramatic, with net worth falling by almost two-thirds, to $6,325.

The main reason for this dramatic decline—though by no means the only reason—relates to housing, or more specifically housing location. Hispanics were hardest hit by the latest recession because they tended to own homes in areas disproportionately affected by home value depreciation, such as Arizona, California, Florida, and Nevada.

Professor Douglas S. Massey of Princeton University has suggested that many Latinos first were victimized by predatory lending and then were dramatically hurt by the drop in construction jobs following the burst of the housing bubble. Regardless of the reasons, the decline has been tragic.

Americans' increasing pessimism. Socioeconomic decline and resulting pessimism is broad-based, but it damages minorities most. First, there is reason for their pessimism. Not only is unemployment for Hispanics in double digits—far higher than it is for non-Hispanics—but also wages for the employed have fallen to a new low. In 1960, personal wages and salary income constituted approximately 52 percent of the gross domestic product, but that number has fallen to less than 44 percent today. The primary result is that the median household income in 2009 was less than it had been more than a decade earlier.

There are very real reasons why many people are feeling pessimistic. In an effort to better understand the American population, the Census Bureau has offered a new income category—the "near poor." The new measure adjusts for cost of living and includes government benefits and income lost to taxes, health care, and work expenses. Under the official measure, 10 percent of the population would fall into the near poor category, while the alternative new measure placed 17 percent of the total population in 2010 in that category. Additionally, the new measure categorized an estimated one-third of the US population as poor, compared with one-fourth of the population under the old measure.

Pessimism and alienation have serious ramifications in both the short term and the long term, and so does perspective. For many Americans, their pessimism is two-pronged: they are not doing well in the new economy, and the nation does not look the way it used to. This is particularly true of white working-class Americans, less than 50 percent of whom identify themselves as "optimistic." In a recent study by the Pew Charitable Trusts' Economic Mobility Project, roughly 66 percent of Latinos and blacks said they expect to be better off in ten years, while only 44 percent of non-college-educated whites felt that way. In another Pew study, when asked if they agreed that "our people are not perfect, but our culture is superior" to that of other countries, 60 percent of those over age fifty agreed, as opposed to only 37 percent of respondents between ages eighteen and twenty-nine. I think this highlights two things: first, the fact that Latinos and blacks have never done as well as whites historically and now see greater opportunity, and, second, those Americans over fifty are old enough to remember times when the United States was stronger both domestically and globally.

In related analysis in the *Los Angeles Times*, Ronald Brownstein cited new research by William Frey who is tracking the "cultural generation gap" or the difference in the percentage of whites between children (under age eighteen) and seniors (over age sixty-five). In 2000, whites constituted about 61 percent of America's children and almost 84 percent of its seniors—a twenty-three-point gap. By 2010 the gap had widened to about twenty-six points, since whites still make up 80 percent of seniors but only 54 percent of children. Of course, the main variable in this equation is the increase in the number of Latino youth, which accelerates the tension in white America over government spending versus government investment. The irony, as Brownstein points out, is that "security for the gray requires opportunity for the brown." After all, someone has to finance Medicare and Social Security.

The future for men. It is clear: men are on the decline and have been affected the most by the recent economic troubles. Recent reports in the *Atlantic* and the *Economist* point out that of the wealthiest seven countries, the United States has the lowest share of "prime age" males who are employed (workers between the ages of twenty-five and fifty-four)—just over 80 percent, compared with 95 percent in the late 1960s. Another way to look at the problem is through real median wages, which have dropped 32 percent in the United States since their peak in 1973.

A prevailing theory is that men who dominated manufacturing jobs shifted to construction as work went overseas, and then construction came to a standstill after the housing bubble burst. Another view is that as the United States struggles to compete globally, it has squeezed out many jobs through increased productivity, which has exacerbated the problem of male unemployment.

Not all problems can be explained away. Don Peck points out in the *Atlantic* that it has long been obvious that blue-collar workers need to get more education or shift to the service side of the economy, but most men have done neither, while women have made the necessary shifts far more easily and in greater numbers. One explanation is that women's "people skills," inclination toward teamwork, and other such attributes are in greater demand in the new economy.

College as a cause for optimism and pessimism. First the good news: The link between college and success is increasingly clear, as in 2011, for the first time in history, more than 30 percent of American adults aged twenty-five and older had at least a bachelor's degree. Latinos also made gains as the number of Latinos with a bachelor's degree or higher grew 80 percent from 2.1 million to 3.8 million between 2001 and 2011. The unemployment rate for college graduates is around 4.2 percent, less than half the unemployment rate for Americans with only a high school degree. Over a lifetime, on average, college graduates will earn almost twice as much as their non-degreed counterparts. Recent research confirms that a college graduate will earn more regardless of the job, even if he or she is working as a cook or secretary.

The bad news is that college graduates fret (for good reason) about not having an advanced or professional degree. In a recent *Wall Street Journal/NBC News* poll, 80 percent of recent graduates said the country is heading in the wrong direction, hurting their future opportunities. Some economic figures support their pessimism: wages fell by 8.6 percent between 2000 and 2010, and the unemployment rate for recent college graduates is 10.7 percent.

These and other factors have led two-thirds of Americans to conclude that their children will not do better than they have. Of course, this is a matter of perspective. If you are the first in your family to graduate from college, even tough times offer new opportunities. On the other hand, as Adam Davidson of *Planet Money* stated in a recent *New York Times* column: "According to many economists, technological advances and competition with low-wage countries, among other factors, portend an America in which the undereducated *everywhere*, including the 85 million people over 25 without postsecondary training, will fall further behind the educated and in-demand software designers and biotech engineers. If that's true, roughly one out of three American workers can expect to see their living standards erode throughout their lifetimes."

There are Opportunities and Bright Spots

The American economy, like the Latino segment within it, has to recognize opportunities early, capitalize on them, and avoid risk aversion at all costs. The subject of immigration and employee mobility offers a perfect example.

According to the new book *Exceptional People: How Migration Shaped Our World and Will Define our Future*, it is estimated that if rich countries were to admit enough migrants from poor countries to expand their own labor force by a mere 3 percent, the world would be richer by $356 billion a year. Completely opening international borders would add $39 trillion over twenty-five years to the global economy.

The same book argues that although immigration is unpopular in rich countries, it should not be—that the impact of immigrants on low-skilled local labor is always exaggerated, and migrants often *create* jobs for native workers.

Another opportunity for which Americans should prepare is the return of some manufacturing to the United States as wages grow by 17 percent a year in China but remain relatively static here. This is critically important, as manufacturing was 25.6 percent of the national GDP in 1950 and had sunk to 11.7 percent by 2010. Yet manufacturing accounts for $1.6 trillion of the American GDP—the same as in China. Some analysts suggest that with some necessary policy adjustments the US could lure some manufacturing from China to the United States, or at a minimum keep pieces of their value-added production chain. Analysts are also warning that the US must prepare its workforce for the return of some manufacturing because Americans have lost many of the critical skills required for those jobs. As a result, according to the *Talent Acquisition Factbook*, manufacturing jobs are the costliest to recruit for—$6,433 for a manufacturing job compared to $2,127 for a health-care job.

In December 2011, Chicago Mayor Rahm Emanuel wrote an op-ed piece in the *Wall Street Journal* highlighting the issue of an overall skills gap. He noted that AAR Corporation, an aviation parts manufacturer in the Chicago area, had six hundred job openings for welders and mechanics but could not find skilled workers to fill them. So, the city is preparing today to fill tomorrow's manufacturing needs by training nine thousand new computer science workers, twenty-thousand new transportation workers, and forty-three thousand new health-care workers, including fifteen thousand nurses, in part by modernizing the community college system.

However, most growth is in the service sector, and that trend will continue for the foreseeable future as it is expected to account for 96 percent of job growth between 2008 and 2018. According to the US Department of Labor, the most jobs generated will be for home and personal care aides, network systems and data communication analysts, financial planners, and biomedical engineers.

Positive signs

Several trends—Latina progress, geographic shifts in the labor market, nearby export markets, and an abundance of low-wage work—all add up to opportunity if Latinos are prepared. It is clear that Latinas have overcome many obstacles to become a dynamic part of the American workforce. In part, this is because Latinas outnumber Latino men in colleges, and their skills are generally better-suited to the new economy, with its focus on services.

A 2011 study of single, childless urban American workers between the ages of twenty-two and thirty found that women in this group earned 8 percent more than men; we can assume Latinas out-earned men in this category although there are no definitive numbers yet. At the same time, there is need for a stronger push to include Latinas in nontraditional lines of work if that is what they choose.

While the Latino move to higher-opportunity areas, particularly the South, has not been without challenges (think immigration laws and blatant discrimination), in general the Latino shift to areas in need of workers is paying off. And as these markets age, youthful Latinos will be seen as a positive economic force.

Robert Pastor of the Center for North American Studies observes that the top two markets for US exports are not China and Germany but its neighbors, Mexico and Canada. The top two sources of energy are not Saudi Arabia and Venezuela; they are Canada and Mexico. These two partners are coming out of the recession more quickly than the US is, and in 2010 alone, American exports to Canada and Mexico increased from $334 billion to $412 billion—more than four times the exports to China, and eight times more than the combined exports to Korea, Colombia, and Panama. It appears that the key to American growth is right next door.

Finally, as a nation people do not want all work to be of the low-wage variety, but some of those jobs are needed. Creating them can have many positive benefits, including moving people off welfare, reducing homelessness, improving work skills, and giving workers an "in" with private employers who can potentially offer other, higher-paying work.

This dynamic is happening in smart communities across the nation and should be expanded, particularly when government contracts are in play. **In a related area, according to the *Economist* there is growing evidence that moderate minimum wage increases are not harmful as many insist, and smaller, more frequent increases are better than America's infrequent but hefty increases. Hopefully there will be minimum wage increases. The lower segment of the workforce has seen its buying power stagnate for much too long. Finally, when are Americans going to recognize that a reasonable "living wage" makes sense for the economy, society, and, particularly, the many young families striving to improve their lives and future?**

We are beginning to understand what it takes to succeed in the new economy and can already see who might be left behind. To be perfectly blunt, what is happening should not be surprising, and it is necessary to heed the signals and respond accordingly. Next, we will move to a macro view of economics with a focus on jobs—how many there are, how many are needed, and the chances of meeting the demand.

Economic Shifts Are Everywhere

There is little argument that these are turbulent times. Whether in the United States, EU nations, Egypt and other Middle Eastern countries, or China, it is clear that there is growing uncertainty about the future of the world and America's ability to cope with it given its people's, and especially its elected officials', apparent inability to manage even today's problems in some coherent fashion. The challenges should be of interest and concern to every American, and particularly to national leaders.

Where the world stands and where it is heading is the focus of great debate among academics, and five books on the subject stand out to me. I will summarize them briefly and then discuss what I consider the most important points.

In *The Great Stagnation*, Tyler Cowen suggests that "America has run out of low-hanging fruit" in the form of free land, immigrant labor, or powerful technologies—that since the seventeenth century, at least, there has been a technological plateau. That is part of the reason for stagnant wages since 1970. He also argues that Americans have fixated on private good at the expense of public good, and that innovation, while interesting, has created comparatively few jobs. (He notes that the iPod has created only 13,920 jobs in the United States.) Cowen sees signs of hope ahead but feels they are tenuous at best.

In *Race Against the Machine: How the Digital Revolution Is Accelerating Innovation, Driving Productivity, and Irreversibly Transforming*

Employment and the Economy, Erik Brynjolfsson focuses on employment, or the lack of it, in the post-recession economy. He notes that many people find the poor employment figures puzzling because economic and business indicators, like the GDP and corporate profits, bounced back from recession relatively quickly. He says the main issue is not cyclicality but stagnation—in this case, an inability to innovate and enhance productivity. Like Cowen, he also points to a technological plateau, a gradual slowdown since 1970 when America's median household income began to slow, in part due to growing competition from China and India. Finally, Brynjolfsson touches on technology's negative impact on job formation—"a race against the machine." Essentially, he says, America is in a Great Restructuring: technologies are racing ahead, but many skills and organizations are lagging. While people cannot win the overall race, he says, they can race with machines.

Paul Gilding, an Australian environmentalist and author of *The Great Disruption*, takes a more integrated but pessimistic view of the future. He interprets global disruptions as signs that the current, growth-obsessed capitalist system is reaching its financial and ecological limits. "Yes, the rich are getting richer and the corporations are making profits," he says, "but meanwhile, the people are getting worse off—drowning in housing debt or tuition debt."

Contrast Gilding's view with that of John Hagel III and John Seely Brown, who, in *The Power of Pull,* see a big shift that integrates globalization and information technology through accelerated flows of ideas, innovation, and collaboration. This shift has the potential to create new opportunities for people around the world the authors say, but it will require wholesale changes in many institutions mired in the past and unprepared for the fast-paced flow of information and changes ahead.

If Americans view the current high unemployment figures as cyclical, and therefore temporary, then they have their heads in the sand, says Jim Clifton, chairman of Gallup. The global war is on, he says, and it is about jobs. In Clifton's new book, *The Coming Jobs War*, he argues that "the primary will of the world is no longer about peace, or freedom, or even democracy; it is not about having a family, and it is neither about God nor owning a home or land. The will of the world is first and foremost to have a good job. Everything else comes after that." He also points out that of the world's five billion people over fifteen years old, three billion said they work or want to work, but there are only 1.2 billion full-time, formal jobs. It is important to keep in mind that Clifton does not raise a high bar: he defines a "good job," also known as a "formal job," as one with a "paycheck from an employer and steady work that averages thirty-plus hours per week." The bottom line for the United States, and every other country, is what share of the world's formal jobs it has acquired.

The jobs challenge for the United States, the EU countries, China, and other advanced countries has become more daunting in light of the growth of emerging states around the world. In 2010, the combined output of the developing economies accounted for 38 percent of the world GDP, and some analysts believe that number will surpass 50 percent in a mere seven years. In 2011, those countries accounted for more than half of global exports, and they were expected to account for over half of all capital spending in 2012. Additionally, these economies accounted for only 17 percent of all outstanding government debt. The developed nations lead in that category.

As the *Economist* stated recently, "Now the tail wags the dog."

Why is this happening? In an article in *Foreign Affairs*, Michael Spence argues that the ascent of these emerging economies is probably permanent and irreversible. They are beating the US at its own game and in areas it previously dominated, like the design and manufacturing of semiconductors, pharmaceuticals, and information technology services.

In some ways, what is more startling is declining exports. Spence notes that between 1990 and 2008, the United States created twenty-seven million jobs, 98 percent of which were in the "non-tradable" sector of the economy—goods and services consumed domestically, such as services provided by the local dry cleaners or power company. By contrast, the tradable sector grew by only six hundred thousand jobs during the same period. At the same time, highly educated Americans are benefiting from employment in the upper end of the value chain, and geared toward products and services that lie within the tradable sector, such as pharmaceuticals and smartphones. Those jobs attract higher compensation than do jobs created only to meet domestic needs.

Overall there is growing evidence that American companies that are innovative and have marketing prowess are globally competitive. While their sales and revenues shine, the jobs for American workers do not follow. Apple is a perfect example: it has a huge market capitalization, growing global revenues—and ten times as many workers employed in China (at lower wages) than in the United States.

Yet the global strategy is still a good one since it is estimated that the center of the world's middle-class spending will shift dramatically in coming decades. For example, North American middle-class spending is projected to grow from $5.5 trillion in 2009 to $5.6 trillion in 2030—a mere blip. At the same time, Asian Pacific countries will see huge gains in middle-class spending, from only $4.9 trillion in 2009 to a staggering $32.9 trillion in 2030.

This dramatic consumer shift in the next decades reaffirms the notion that the United States must continue to advance the best technological thinking. But in some ways, creativity and innovation may be even more important since the best bet is to produce more attractive products than people in other countries can buy from companies on their own continents. After all, products with flair, from companies like Apple, Levis, and Nike, are desired even by people in emerging countries.

Ironically, the United States is looking more like Europe all the time. The American employment rate is only slightly higher than that of Europe as a whole, and it is below that of Germany. US youth unemployment is approaching the European level, and long-term unemployment is rising almost as quickly here as it is in Spain although the percentage is smaller overall. Youth unemployment is particularly disturbing because the "scarring effects" linger, with serious, predictable socioeconomic repercussions: accelerated benefit payments, lost income tax revenues, wasted capacity, long-term wage losses, cultural alienation, unemployment-related unhappiness, and fewer stable families.

So why are jobs vanishing and so hard to create? Don Peck in the *Atlantic* notes that the American economy has been in a sea change for more than thirty years, shifting from manufacturing to services and information, and integrating itself far more tightly into a single, global market for goods, labor, and capital. Peck cites a Federal Reserve report estimating that between 20 and 22 percent of American jobs could move overseas within the next two decades.

Add to these overall trends the fact that, in order to compete in the global marketplace, American businesses have become ever more efficient by outsourcing jobs to lower-wage countries; pushing worker productivity to the limit; reducing the rate at which they add new employees; and incorporating more computerization and mechanization. As former Labor Secretary Robert Reich has observed, it is a good time to be a consumer, but a tough time to be a worker.

It is also becoming clear that there are huge pay variations even within the same professions. According to Adam Davidson of *Planet Money*, registered nurses are a good example of this phenomenon: a senior nurse in a doctor's office earns $112,500, a mid-career nurse in a private hospital earns $66,650, an on-site nurse at an amusement park earns $43,050, and a school nurse at a state junior college earns $28,950.

All these factors add up to constant pressure on American workers to learn and utilize skills that cannot be easily duplicated by computers and other technology or to pursue careers that cannot be outsourced to lower-wage countries (think firemen, plumbers, or heart surgeons). Historically the best-protected jobs have been in the service sector, but even some of that work has been off-shored. Accounting and select legal work are high-end examples.

Maybe the future of the American worker is brighter than many believe, and maybe it is not. We can only prepare ourselves, which is ultimately the focus of this book. Latinos and other Americans must continue to prepare for a changing and more competitive world. As we will see in the next chapter, Americans are increasingly connected to and dependent upon one another, particularly as the population ages.

A Perspective on the Future

The United States has been the world's largest economy since the 1890s, and, although a horrific decline is not imminent, Americans now face serious challenges. Certainly it would be foolish to look to the past to predict the future. The main challenger to US economic dominance is China, whose economy has grown seven times faster than ours over the past decade and is predicted to be the world's largest by 2016. The other BRIC nations (Brazil, Russia, India), along with other emerging markets both large and small, represent another, collective economic challenge.

It is generally argued that the United States is in decline to some degree. In a recent survey of Harvard Business School alumni, 71 percent agree there has been a decline in American competitiveness. Additionally, according to the National Commission on Adult Literacy, ninety million adults have such inadequate literacy skills that their chances of success in postsecondary education and training are greatly compromised; there are as many as three million job openings because of a serious skills gap in the American workforce. At the same time, the emerging nations are "upping their game," notes author and analyst Fareed Zakaria. They are challenging the US in areas it once dominated. Prosperity in the world is, of course, a good thing—it means more people to sell to and, in the long run, a reduction in armed conflicts, environmental degradation (as per capita income increases), and human rights abuses. But the average American views these changes in negative terms, as the country and economy have faltered.

Challenges and Opportunities

Here are just a few of the critical issues the nation will be struggling with in the decades ahead:

Income. The average American has seen his or her earning power and income reduced. Between 1946 and 1973, per capita household income grew 100 percent; between 1973 and 2004, it grew just 22 percent; between 2000 and 2010, it actually declined.

Aging. In 2011, the first group of baby boomers reached the age of sixty-five and became eligible for Medicare; seventy-nine million more will follow over the next eighteen years. That is a significant number of people leaving the labor force and moving into the entitlement years of Medicare and Social Security. Though many baby boomers will work longer than they anticipated, the economy will still lose many qualified workers or see older workers remain in the workforce reluctantly.

Births. Like all advanced economies, the United States will see its population growth slow, although it will still reach 438 million by 2050 (up from 303 million in 2012). This is, of course, due to greater longevity and not more births. For some time now, birth rates have been declining all over the world, with the exception of the poor nations in sub-Saharan Africa, South Asia, and parts of the Middle East and North Africa.

Race and ethnicity. Between 2012 and 2050, the percentage of whites in the United States will have declined to 47 percent of the total population. Blacks will remain 13 percent, while Asians will grow to 9 percent. Hispanics will more than double their current share, to 29 percent.

Rising costs. In 2011, the US government spent $1.56 trillion on Medicare, Medicaid, and Social Security benefits—more than $4 billion a day. In 2022, if no changes are made, the government will spend just under $3 trillion annually on these programs, or 54 percent of the expected federal budget.

Working-age "payers." According to PERE at USC, the gap between the number of working-age people and the children and seniors who depend on them will grow. In 2005 there were fifty-nine children or seniors for every one hundred workers; in 2050, there will be seventy-two.

Conclusion. Simply put, the rich nations are growing older, putting them at domestic and international disadvantage. The Latino population offers the US economy a demographic opportunity.

Response. It would be wise to prepare this segment of America to deliver for the country. I believe strongly that investing in a nation's people is both smart and just. Yet as I read the tea leaves, I see economic, fiscal, and political challenges that will lead to a decrease in this kind of investment on the part of government. Communities, neighborhoods, and especially families will be challenged to do more than they ever have in order to lift themselves up. It will require everyone to work harder, but collective success will not come if it is not done smartly. Thinking will make the difference, and that is the focus of the next chapter.

Growing Share of Enrollment

Figure 1.1 Hispanic Share of Pre-K through 12th Grade Public School Enrollment and 18- to 24-Year-Old College Enrollment, 1972-2011

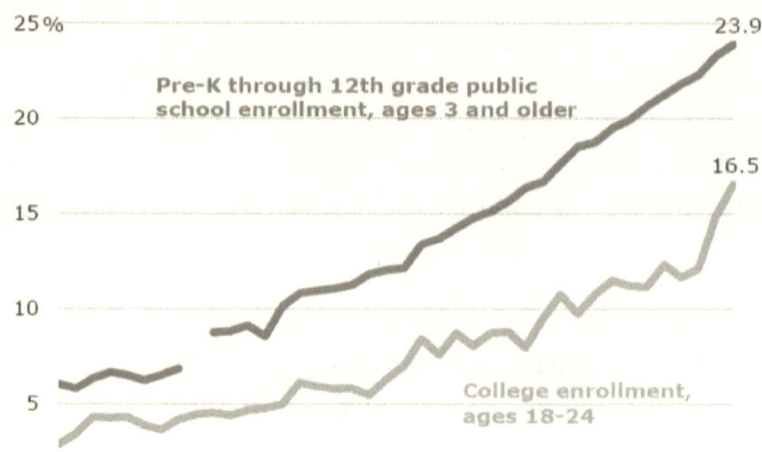

Notes: "Pre-K through 12th grade public school enrollment, ages 3 and older" shows the Hispanic share of enrollment in public schools from pre-K through 12th grade. Public school enrollment figures for 1980 are not available. "College enrollment, ages 18-24" shows Hispanic share among college students ages 18 to 24.

Source: Pew Hispanic Center analysis of the October Current Population Survey (CPS)

Thinking and Finding Answers

It is unquestionably true that Latinos are hard workers. They always have been, and they continue to demonstrate a work ethic that compares favorably with that of any segment of the population. So far this has served them well, but in an information and technology-driven world, work ethic will not be enough. As time goes on, work ethic will have to be matched by critical thinking—that is how individual, family, and community progress will be achieved. And while that progress might be led by community leaders, strong and useful thinking can come from anyone. Take an insight, which is simply a different way of looking at something that has been in plain sight forever, and through that, new approaches can be advanced. Anyone can come up with an insight. In fact, the best insights often do not come from experts.

I would argue that, to see more progress ahead, Latinos will also need help from government at all levels. This is not unusual in US history, and today Latinos cannot allow the public sector to avoid its traditional role. At the same time, the Latino community will need to understand American society through a broader contextual lens, for if Latinos understand the challenges and opportunities in the nation, they can adapt to and participate in the opportunities ahead.

Critical thinking can allow people to understand and embrace the new and smart thinking happening all around. For example, all people recognize that the world has changed dramatically in the last twenty-plus years, but many do not understand the scope of that change; most people have a sense of only what is happening on the surface. Increased connectivity through smartphones and other technology is an obvious example. Most people do not know that phone data is collected and used to figure out voting patterns; to pinpoint which low-income areas are generating spending and offer opportunities for economic development; or even to identify areas with growing rates of mental illness. If Latinos do not understand this, how can communities more fully embrace this technology to improve individual and collective well-being? In fact, residents of Latino neighborhoods have many ways to connect and support one another through new phone technology. Moving forward, I believe this sort of connectivity is critical to a strategic development approach.

It is an insightful understanding of significant changes and new ideas that is behind the advancement of countries like Singapore, companies like Google, products like the iPhone, and concepts like "the 99 percent." The nation's best thinkers should lead the way in these areas, but everyone can and should learn what is happening for themselves, their families, and their communities.

Latinos need to understand that information is cheap but knowledge expensive. The overall value and power of clarity is essential. Sergey Brin and Larry Page, founders of Google, once said, "We deliver the world's information in one click." There is power in that message.

Latinos need to understand and accept the growing role of women. They have many of the skills (and the temperament) valued in the new economy and control 51 percent of private wealth in the United States.

Latinos need to understand that words matter, whether the concept is simple (a *quiz* is better received than a *test*) or complex (as in *climate change* versus *global warming*).

Latinos must also discover what their communities are all about. Master Lock figured out that its business is not really about locks, but about what those locks protect. Similarly, for better or worse, European citizens have apparently decided that they support a market economy, but not a market society—meaning they still wants a stronger support structure for everyone.

Everyone must be made aware that Latinos and other minorities are on the wrong side of the digital divide, which means they are out of sync with the direction the world is taking potentially affecting the nation's productivity.

Latinos need to understand that in today's world, where you live and work matters, and improving and protecting those places is important. In this case, it is neighborhoods.

Finally, anything can change, even the most deep-seated traditions. Shaadi.com is a highly successful Internet marriage service in India that has introduced 1.4 million couples. This is an ever-changing world.

Peter Drucker, the legendary management thinker, has written about "the future that's already happened." In other words, there is often a lag between the evidence of change in a business or society and the broad acceptance of that change. Those who wait for all the evidence to come in will always find themselves behind the curve.

Latinos are a future that has already happened. The community needs to live up to that reality.

Thinking about Thinking

It is called the "knowledge economy" for a reason: the best thinking generates ideas, which generate answers which in turn generates profit.

We need to build a strategic intellectual foundation upon which innovative thinking and ideas can lead to action that will help change the trajectory of Latino progress.

This section of the book is about thinking. The next is about ideas and answers.

There is growing research about the brain, what it generates, and how it generates so many great concepts, ideas, and thoughts. I cannot do the entire subject justice here, but it is critically important to at least touch on this area as part of the overall approach of this book. The intent is twofold: first, to reinforce how valuable the input of many people can be in generating smart answers to family development; and second, to challenge people in neighborhoods across the country to commit to the same level of thinking. It will make a difference.

Thoughts on Thinking

Everything you need exists. As the book *Smart World* points out, throughout history the great thinkers, innovators, and inventors had a unique ability to see a problem in broad terms, recognize the existing elements of a solution, and then combine them in ways no one had thought of before. Gutenberg did this with the printing press; so did Steve Jobs with Apple. This suggests that seeing broadly is a talent—and that the old criticism "He's an inch deep and a mile wide" might need to be reevaluated.

When contemplating how to support Latino families, therefore, it is important to remember that the challenge is not about inventing one new thing; it is about combining what exists to meet the challenges families face in today's world. Can neighborhood watch efforts be improved by linking them to smartphones? Can local parks be better utilized by linking them to farmers markets? Or can residents be linked to local businesses in new ways that benefit both? With a little thought the possibilities are enormous.

Less is more. In contemporary society too often complex thinking is admired. Steven J. Paley, an inventor and the author of *The Art of Invention: The Creative Process of Discovery and Design*, notes that "simplicity is always something to strive for" and "it is much easier to add complexity than to work and discover simplicity." He defines simplicity as doing the most with the least and offers as an example the paper clip: a wire, with three bends.

Latino neighborhoods should be filled with men and women selling a range of products and services door-to-door. This saves residents time and offers a business opportunity to fellow neighbors. It is a simple idea that is decades old and still works.

This book will advance ideas and approaches that some will consider too simple and thus unimportant. This could not be further from the truth. Consider all the small things you remember because, in some way, they changed your life for the better.

We need to learn the process. David Kelley, the founder of the design firm IDEO, has said that anyone can be creative—they just have to learn how. His particular design process is to thoughtfully define a problem; visualize it and brainstorm to come up with possible solutions; and then create a prototype. He also believes that collaborating with others is how people learn best. He says a new process is required if people want to complete something quickly, accurately, and efficiently. As it turns out, process even guides creativity!

Everyone can participate. The book *The Innovator's DNA* (Christensen, Dyer, Gregersen) promotes the concept that to "think different" you have to act different, and that five "discovery skills" are part of an innovator's makeup. Interestingly, one of the skills—making connections across fields—is cognitive, while the other four—questioning, observing, networking, and experimenting—are behavioral. The authors conclude that almost everyone has some capacity for creativity and innovative thinking.

Everyone has ideas because everyone has a unique perspective on any given situation. Latinos should look to their peers for ideas, consider them seriously, and understand how to link them to other ideas.

Finding the Right Answers

It has become clear that the ideas that drive community development generally have been dominated by social sector thinking. Moving forward, it will be critical to incorporate ideas from the social, government, and private sectors as well as from involved individuals. All offer unique perspectives and expertise. Bringing these perspectives to the planning process and seriously considering them can generate new approaches to problems that offer a chance for greater overall impact on Latino communities.

In that spirit, I will review some new insights and approaches that may lead to innovative ways to help Latino families progress significantly in a single generation.

Decision fatigue. An essay in the book *Willpower: Rediscovering the Greatest Human Strength* observes that good decision making is not a trait—in other words, it is not a constant state but one that fluctuates. That fluctuation occurs in part because of "decision fatigue." People have a finite store of mental energy for exerting self-control. This is a serious problem for the poor, who are constantly expending that mental energy due to a lack of financial resources. For poor people, a trip to the supermarket is an exhausting series of compromises and adjustments which are compounded throughout the day. Many Latinos, particularly women, find themselves in this challenging situation. Local programs that help families budget and manage their purchasing should be readily available and could help many.

Smartphones. These phones are tools not just for users but for researchers as well. Phone company data on the use of smartphones can reveal subtle symptoms of mental illness, foretell movements in the Dow Jones Industrial Average, or chart the spread of political ideas as they move through a community. Researchers are exploring how to use such data to improve public health, urban planning, and (of course) marketing. One researcher uses global phone data to determine how slums can be a catalyst for a city's economic vitality. I am convinced that smartphones have dramatic potential to help Latino families within neighborhoods connect with each other, not just to find support but also to advance their collective involvement with the so-called informal economy through bartering, selling, and sharing products and services. After all, Latino smartphone ownership has jumped from roughly 10 percent to 35 percent in four years.

Collective thinking. Change and invention are no longer the domains of individual genius but of loosely coordinated and potentially global crowds of citizens. People from around the world have come together to produce an innovative online encyclopedia (Wikipedia) and to monitor the skies from their amateur telescopes in order to expand collective understanding of the universe. These organizations, which fall under the banner of "crowd sourcing," bring together a range of perspectives with the recognition that the *wisdom of crowds* is just that—wise. The potential to use this approach in Latino neighborhoods is enormous, and it is the basis for much of the strategy outlined in this book, particularly in the area of neighborhood planning.

Reliance on the practical. By making simple, practical changes, researchers at Cornell University redesigned school cafeterias at minimal cost with dramatic results. When they gave healthy foods more descriptive names, for example, *creamy corn* rather than *corn*, sales increased by 27 percent. When cafeteria workers asked each child, "Do you want a salad?", salad sales increased by a third. When they put apples and oranges in a fruit bowl rather than a stainless steel pan, fruit sales more than doubled. The application for Latinos? They have the propensity for hypertension, in part because they use too much salt. Removing the salt shaker from the proverbial table and buying fewer prepackaged foods, which invariably contain more sodium, can improve health dramatically.

Behavioral economics. Researchers can generally predict how people will behave in certain situations, and through behavioral economics people can use that knowledge to promote better choices. Researchers know that you consider yourself above average because almost everyone considers himself above average—like the 90 percent of drivers who think they are good drivers. They also know that if you have fat friends you will probably become fat; that you will generally live with the status quo (as in leaving your 401k exactly where it is); and that if you discuss flossing your teeth one week, you will floss more the next. All people—even judges—are influenced by their peers

So if behavioral scientists know how to nudge people to do the right thing for themselves and society, why do they not do it more often? All this science is not commonly known, so Latino leaders, officials, parents, and families must learn more about it. Sometimes very simple strategies can convince teens not to smoke, encourage girls not to get pregnant, convey the benefits of looking and being smart, or warn of the perils of gang membership.

These chapters have focused on the need for Latinos to think as hard as they work. That means understanding the environment within which everyone operates and recognizing the triggers that can advance Latino thinking: using existing tools in new combinations; embracing the power of simple solutions; maximizing new tools like smartphones; and learning how to nudge people—particularly young people—into making the right choices. Later chapters will show how these approaches can be used to advance families and the neighborhoods in which they live.

Now we turn to focus on Latinos and some of their cultural traits—some of which will be well-accepted in American society, while others might not.

How Do Latinos See Themselves?

This book is about Latino progress, with an emphasis on the next generation, and about why Latinos are in many ways unprepared for the rapid changes in the economy and society. I have outlined how progress has been made more challenging by issues of timing—the fact that most Latinos entered the country primarily after the foundational years of post-World War II and were affected by seismic socioeconomic shifts beyond anyone's control. Nevertheless, Latinos have been, and will continue to be, responsible for their own future. If that future is to be a successful one, individual Latinos, their families, and the broader community must make a serious self-assessment—not only because it requires honest introspection, but also because it contributes to strategic thinking about individual and collective advancement.

It is important to recognize that the fifty million Latinos living in this country are not monolithic but have much in common culturally and often historically. Many, but not all, Latinos live in primarily Latino neighborhoods, hear or speak Spanish daily, share common media, demonstrate cultural similarities, interact with institutions in similar ways, share the same socioeconomic characteristics as their neighbors, and cling to the desire to improve their lives as dramatically and quickly as possible.

So, in many ways, Latinos do have a collective past, present, and future.

Almost all of America is hurting. The broader, more established part of American society seems to have accepted the idea that they may not do better than their parents. Stunningly, 60 percent of workers aged fifty-five or older have less than $100,000 in a retirement account, according to the Employee Benefit Research Institute. So to assume that the older, more established portion of the American population will embrace the emerging Latino population financially is in some ways a reach. Latinos can advance only if they meet the challenges and standards imposed on everyone while also maintaining their family and community culture and traditions. While this strategy has been and continues to be achievable, it is time for the Latino community to make a candid assessment of its place in this complex but important space.

A Critical Self-Assessment

Oscar Arias, president of Costa Rica from 1986 to 1990 and 2006 to 2010, gave just this sort of honest assessment in a 2011 *Foreign Affairs* article, "Culture Matters," in which he theorized why Latin American countries have tended to lag behind other developed countries in other parts of the world.

He was quick to reject theories with conspiratorial undertones, such as the argument that the Spanish empire made off with the area's riches in the past, or that the American empire supposedly continues to bleed it dry. He also dismissed contentions that international financial institutions have schemed to hold Latin America back and that globalization was deliberately designed to keep the region in the shadows.

While acknowledging that other countries have affected Latin America's fate, Arias promotes a theory that he says applies to all nations, and he recalls Latin America's historical prominence (subsequently lost) going back to the fifteenth century.

With that foundation, Arias describes four obstacles to the progress of Latin America. The first, he says, is the fact that "Latin Americans glorify their past so ceaselessly that they make it almost impossible to advocate change …[They would rather] hold on tight even to pain and suffering, preferring a certain present to an uncertain future."

The second obstacle is lack of confidence. Arias considers Latin Americans to be among the most distrustful people in the world, and he supports that contention with research comparing their attitude to that of Europeans. One startling statistic is that only 3 percent of Brazilians said yes to the question "Can most people be trusted?"

The third obstacle blocking development, he says, is the fragility of the Latin American commitment to democracy. He argues that "after centuries of civil wars, coups, and dictators, democracy has indeed made remarkable strides in recent decades," yet still it yields to authoritarianism.

Finally, Arias makes the simple but powerful argument that Latin America has never established a culture of peace. He notes that while the only Latin American country facing imminent or ongoing conflict is Colombia, the region still spends $60 billion dollars annually on armaments—money that could instead be used to address hunger, illiteracy, inequality, environmental degradation, and other societal ills.

Arias sets a high standard for candor, one that many people around the world, including the US Latino population, should emulate. His tone is not self-loathing but conveys his honest intent to build positively on reality rather than on feel-good falsehoods.

In "From Farmingville to East Hampton," posted in January 2008 on the Yahoo! Contributor Network, John Meyers provides interesting insight into Latino culture from an outside perspective as he explains why an affluent neighborhood in the Northeast was so annoyed with new immigrants. At issue, he writes, was a clash of cultural values.

Meyers describes Latinos as people whose worldview is shaped by their culture and their religion, both of which permeate their daily lives. The stereotypical Mañana Syndrome is real, he says, but it revolves around placing people over time schedules. He notes that Latinos are collective rather than individualistic thinkers, respecting hierarchy, status, and collective culture and avoiding taboo subjects. He concludes that many people probably find Latinos odd because they tend to communicate through body language, both indirectly and deliberately.

Is Meyers's assessment correct? It depends who you ask. Some of his conclusions would garner nods of approval, while others might be considered outdated—and then there are shades of gray throughout his analysis. But I would say the approach is fair. With that in mind, I will follow with my thoughts on what this sort of cultural clash means for Latinos going forward.

The Implications for Family and Neighborhood Development

It is best to approach this important but complex (and often emotional) topic with as little moral judgment as possible, relying on independent thought and embracing broad context as a guide. Quite simply, the purpose of this analysis is to explore how the dominant Latino cultural characteristics can help, hurt, or be inconsequential when it comes to the overarching goal of this book: to prepare Latino children for mainstream success in one generation. In my view, this goal warrants an honest and thoughtful assessment with relevant conclusions.

Clearly there are strengths and weaknesses built into the culture of any society, and Hispanic society is no different. Maybe the critical question is, "What cultural traits should Latinos maintain, adjust, or eliminate in order to advance in American society?" The question itself may be too provocative to lead to constructive discussion within the greater Latino community, but I guarantee it is on the minds of many Americans in general, and it is a critical issue.

Here is my assessment given the context outlined above:

When Latino culture and religion become the basis for a worldview, they might create a strong personal foundation, but they can also lead to rigidity that squelches a broader, nuanced view of a changing and complex world. A better idea is to combine traditional cultural/religious views with new ideas and beliefs. Those can be compatible concepts, and they would allow Latinos to better adjust to societal changes and evolving issues, from the role of women to gay rights and beyond.

Latinos' respect for hierarchy and status has an "old world" distinction that is losing prominence in a modern world, particularly in the United States where they have tried to hold on to the idea that people are equal and can move beyond whatever station in life they are born into. In fact, Americans have held on to this idea even as social advancement appears more difficult than ever. The bottom line is that Latino families should always believe their members are as good as anyone.

Given that American culture is highly individualistic, the Latino collectivist approach puzzles many Americans. However, their skepticism may change as what I think of as a "societal reset" takes hold, and many people are realizing that Latinos need strong families and communities in order to navigate an increasingly challenging economy and build better futures.

Group avoidance (with the exception of family) is a trait that has often been attributed to Latino culture, and the implications of that trait are significant in this networked world where people must build connections in order to compete. Now no one is an island—everyone must become involved with their neighborhood and community. This shift could be vital to the advancement of Latinos in neighborhoods throughout the country

The nuanced communication style shared by Latinos and some other minority populations baffles some Americans. The tendency to be deliberate, nonverbal, and even indirect is accepted in many parts of the world, but not so much in the United States. While the direct American approach can be heavy-handed and abrupt, it is the norm. And given the importance of human interaction to socioeconomic success, it is important.

The growing role of women and the decline of the macho factor in Latino society are two trends that must continue. Latinas are doing everything that women in broader American society are doing. If some Latino men do not recognize that fact, they may be the last to know.

Finally, the commitment to family is a clear Latino advantage, but it needs to be as thoughtful as it is emotional. A father can love his children intensely but then make one or all of them leave school early to get a job. Even in hard times, that is a failing strategy that will doom any young person.

What conclusions can you draw from this? Be clear about the culture on which you stake your future. If you choose to accept certain traits and reject others, be certain that the traits you embrace are ones that allow your children the chance to succeed in American society.

As I move closer to a greater strategic framework for advancing Latino progress, I will review my thinking behind that strategy. I will also explain why they must take a counterintuitive approach, guided by a clear understanding of the environment in which they operate.

Collar Disparity
Total Share of Occupation for Higher Degree of Education: 2003 & 2011

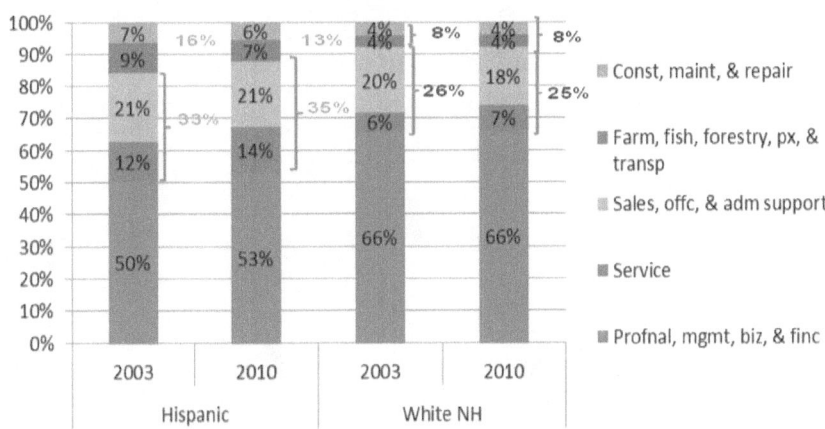

White Collar: Professional, management, business, and financial.
Gray Collar: Service, sales, office and administrative support.
Blue Collar: Construction, maintenance, repair, farming, fishing, forestry, production and transportation.

Hispanics with any type of college degree have made some improvement in moving 3 pts. into white collar occupations while WNH have stayed flat; a huge gap remains as Hispanics are 20% less likely to hold white collar jobs.

The Future That's
Already Happened

Peter Drucker's concept of "the future that's already happened" in many ways seems meant for the role the Latino community can play in the future of America. In order to achieve positive results, it will have to make a big push for progress, but it will be worth the effort.

The Latino community's progress as a vital element of this nation's future will require commitment, cooperation, and hard work. More than anything though, it will necessitate in-depth, creative, strategic thinking—the kind outlined in earlier chapters of this book. Those sections were meant to send a clear message: there can be nothing casual in planning a new strategy to advance areas like education, skills, wealth creation, and overall family progress. This book outlines ideas that can be followed at the neighborhood level by Latinos of all backgrounds.

But a project which involves literally millions of people and thousands of communities requires an innovative foundation in and of itself. And while the scale of the overall effort might be startling to some people and seem less than concrete initially, it proves viable if viewed as an evolving process.

Such an approach is unique and might make some people uncomfortable, but as a response to an unpredictable world and future, it is realistic. In her thoughtful book *The Future and Its Enemies*, Virginia Postrel focuses on "statists," people who are afraid of the future and advocate for greater controls to protect people from it. Conversely,

Postrel advances the idea that people need to build upon the changes they see and that people have an unknown but positive future—if the statists will get out of the way. She quotes the historian and philosopher of science, Stephen Toulmin: "All we can be called upon to do is to take a start from where we are, at the time we are there …There is no way of cutting ourselves free of our conceptual inheritance: all we are required to do is use our experience critically and discriminately, refining and improving our inherited ideas, and determining more exactly the limits of their scope." The title of Postrel's book is appropriate, too. People are the future, but they also have enemies, mostly in the form of changing economic dynamics.

An excellent, more recent book, *Obliquity: Why Our Goals Are Best Achieved Indirectly*, follows a similar but unique view. Author John Kay quotes George Merck, founder of one of the greatest pharmaceutical companies: "We try to never forget that medicine is for people. It is not for the profits. The profits follow, and if we have remembered that, they have never failed to appear. The better we have remembered it, the larger they have been." Companies that have embodied that indirect approach to success also include Johnson & Johnson, GE, and Sony, among others.

Obliquity contrasts two methods of problem solving: direct and indirect (or "oblique"). The direct problem solver reviews all possible outcomes; the oblique problem solver chooses from a much more limited set. The direct problem solver assembles all available information; the oblique problem solver recognizes the limits of his or her knowledge. The direct problem solver always finds an explanation for his or her choice; the oblique problem solver sometimes just finds the right choice.

In an uncertain environment, there are no certain choices; different people will perceive the same choices differently. Politicians and policy makers often put on a show of describing their objectives, evaluating their options, and reviewing all the evidence, but in reality their evaluations are dictated by their conclusions, and policy-based evidence supplants evidence-based policy. Take the building of sports stadiums: while officials continually tout the financial impact of these projects, the evidence suggests that in many cases the numbers just do not hold up, and the projects end up costing taxpayers millions of dollars.

It is this kind of insight, along with the kind of critical thinking described earlier in this book, that has too often been lacking in the past, and that must form the foundation of strategic planning and implementation at the local level.

The US operates as a knowledge economy, and success is all about creativity and ideas. In this sort of environment, connectedness is critical: everyone has ideas and insights and can contribute to the collective future.

If researchers can understand better than ever how people think, communities can use that knowledge to develop new tools and use them in innovative ways with tremendous success.

Above all, Latinos need clarity.

Clarity about how the world is changing.

Clarity about the past, the "timing" issue, and what could have been done differently over the past decades to increase the odds of success.

Clarity about the effects of the recent recession and how it has set back the Latino community.

And everyone needs to be honest in self-assessment and ready to break with the past and generate new strengths that historically have been weaknesses, such as cooperation. Most of all, Latinos need to find the best answers to advance community progress. Average will not do.

As a young and growing population, Latinos can play an important role in the nation's future. But the challenge will be great because, as of today, they are not prepared from an educational standpoint—a problem that likely will be exacerbated by the government's budget troubles. The result? To advance, the Latino community and its families will be forced to progress with fewer resources than previous generations.

The plan laid out in this book is in many ways unconventional, but it is a response to unconventional times. Wish for a different situation will not make it so. In the coming pages I will outline how the obliquity approach can be used to achieve the overarching goal of the book.

Moving Forward

"Thinking is easy, acting is difficult, and to put one's thoughts into action is the most difficult thing in the world."

Johann Wolfgang von Goethe

While it is true that acting is difficult, thinking is not easy both if you are trying to understand a macro-level problem and consider it critically within the larger context of a complex and changing world. Add to that challenge the desire (and, ultimately, the need) to offer an unconventional plan in keeping with the gravity of the situation. And the situation is grave: I believe this is a pivotal point for the nation's Latino community. The economy is increasingly competitive, advanced education and job skills are becoming critical to success, and the nation's middle class is shrinking—all these things are happening while the Latino community continues to operate in catch-up mode.

So yes, it is difficult to put one's thoughts into action, and even more difficult to put unconventional thoughts into action, but that is the challenge today. In fact, if this vision for change entails anything less than an unconventional approach, the broader community is being sold short. Yet the three pillars that must hold up this effort are absolutely conventional: good intentions, critical thinking, and a commitment to follow-through.

And while it may be comforting to imagine that a vision and a plan can remain static long enough for people to understand its nuances, that is not the case. Things are changing too quickly, and it is essential to monitor the changes, big and small. For example, it was previously logical to suggest that people track where the jobs are and move there. Sitting in a Latino policy meeting just a few short years ago, I suggested that not everyone could afford to live in the Sunbelt, with its high cost of living (particularly housing)—that there were unfilled jobs and cheaper homes and apartments in more remote locations. Now that philosophy has changed. The current view is that if you have no specialized skills, it is not smart to uproot family and become last in line for jobs that people in the area have coveted for some time. In doing so you also incur moving costs and lose the network of people who know your skills and work ethic and so might be able to help you acquire a new and better job.

Mean Household Income

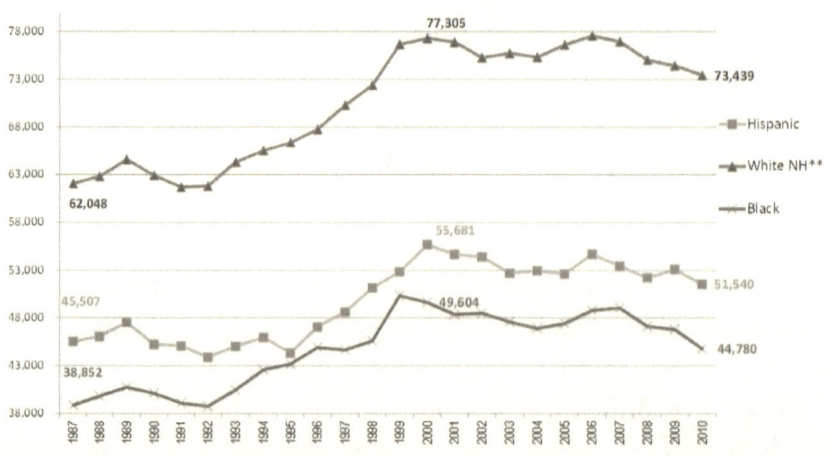

Source: Current Population Survey: Mean HH Income 1987-2010 (Adjusted to 2010 dollars)

The disparity in mean household income between Hispanic and White NH exceeds $20,000.

Though there is plenty of uncertainty in a complicated economy, it should not prevent envisioning new ideas for and approaches to progress. There are still plenty of unknowns, including what makes individuals, families, and neighborhoods successful in a range of areas, from health to education to finances to family relations. Latinos must heed this knowledge and not reinvent where reinvention is unnecessary. Since many Latinos are entrepreneurial, I will offer a business-related example:

Small businesses fail at an alarming rate, and while this is inevitable in a capitalist society, it is also often preventable. There are at least nine reasons why entrepreneurs so often fail: (1) They are undercapitalized from the outset; (2) They do not organize as corporations, but as sole proprietorships; (3) They often have no formal business plan; (4) They prefer not to take over an existing business; (5) They avoid business-to-business operations in favor of business-to-consumer; (6) They often chase the same consumers as already successful businesses; (7) They underemphasize marketing; (8) They pay scant attention to financial controls; (9) They try to compete on price.

That is a long list of known issues that experts have identified as seriously problematic for small business, and while not all of them are avoidable, many are—yet small businesses plunge ahead, apparently thinking they are different. They are not, and to be honest, neither are Latinos.

My point? That Latinos should listen to the experts, particularly in areas we know little about, and take note of the research and recommendations that are all around.

But there is a hitch.

Latinos should heed the core advice that doctors having been giving all Americans for decades—you know, eat healthy foods, exercise, do not smoke, and do not drink, or only drink in moderation. With a little willpower, that strategy is easy enough for most people to follow. But what about poor Latinos, especially those living in "urban deserts" where food is expensive and fresh fruits and vegetables are particularly difficult to find on a regular basis?

People often know the right things to do in a range of areas, but they will not—or cannot—do them.

Everyone needs to help make it easier for Latinos to do the right things. In the case of urban deserts, promoting farmers markets while enlisting the support of major food retailers, smaller independents, and food inspectors to ensure that poorer areas receive fresh fruit and produce at a fair price is a good place to start.

When considering goals, strategies, and innovative approaches to advance the well-being of Latino families, it is important to remember the issues and challenges already discussed—not because Latinos should operate entirely in reactive mode, but because Latinos have to know who they are, what they have been through, and where the community's strengths and challenges lie.

At the beginning of this book, I outlined the opportunities specific to post-World War II America and how at that point in history the Latino population was quite small. These were foundational years for most Americans, and the fact that significant Latino growth occurred after this golden era became what I call a "timing issue" because Latinos had no opportunity to transition into the new, knowledge-based economy. This is part of the reason many Latinos are still of low socioeconomic status.

I described how the tremendous growth of the Latino population since the early 1980s changed the country's dynamics in a way that was critical but not immediately understood. Demographic analysis, one of the few precise forecasters of a changing world, predicted that America's Latino population would grow due to immigration and birth rates and remain relatively young. Non-Latino populations, on the other hand, were already aging and would continue to do so for many years. The implications of this shift, though clear, were ignored by many.

We then moved to a discussion of the current global economy, which is facing both structural and cyclical challenges as rich nations age and poor countries remain youthful. The impact on the United States is clear in some areas and murky in others. While the United States is not immune to global changes, it also faces some unique issues that have left many in a quandary, including generational progress, the decline of the middle class, and international competitiveness, to name a few.

We explored how, in a hypercompetitive world, critical thinking is essential to achieving the best solutions to pressing problems. Fortunately, every member of a community can contribute fresh thoughts and perspectives; with enough awareness, there really is a democracy of ideas.

I then moved to an assessment of Latino culture and how it offers tools Latinos can use and, in some cases, obstacles they must avoid if they are to progress and be key players in the nation's future.

I closed with a plea for all Latinos to understand and embrace clarity on the variables that are critical to their futures.

These issues, insights, and analyses inform and drive the plan which follows.

The Goal:

To help Latino families prepare their children for mainstream success in one generation. This means they will have *knowledge/skills, understanding, and confidence, and a plan to build upon and advance.*

Knowledge continues to be associated with higher education, particularly advanced degrees, but **skills**—critical thinking combined with industry-specific requirements—also produce long-term opportunities.

Understanding can apply to anything from education requirements, university choices, career opportunities, and financial aid options, to how to make and use contacts to advance in a networked world.

Confidence—or the lack thereof—has held back scores of bright Latinos who have been discouraged by teachers, family members, or community contacts. Even if they achieve academic success in high school or college, many Latino students still never reach their highest potential.

Plans are particularly important for young people whose families have a limited educational background. Even a rudimentary plan reinforces in their mind, and the minds of others, that they can expect to achieve more than society might expect of them.

You might wonder why the overarching goal of this book is so specific—that is, having children prepared for mainstream success in one generation. Why not focus on improving household income? Why not advance both parents and children? Why not move everyone up the socioeconomic ladder? Why not improve education for everyone in the home? All these questions are logical, but they do not reflect oblique thinking.

By targeting mainstream success in a single generation, this plan is designed to *indirectly* address all these issues because attaining the goal requires overall family progress that anticipates, solves, and minimizes potential problems and maximizes opportunities.

Getting to Strategies and Programs

There are three types of organizations best exemplified in the business world. The first type, which represents the vast majority, is mainstream and conventional and simply hopes to improve a little each year. The second type does what others do but in a different way, like Southwest Airlines. The last type, a very small minority, does breakthrough, innovative work: think Apple and Google.

In this plan I hope Latinos will occupy that middle space—doing what others attempt to do, but in different ways and on a larger scale. During the planning process, I attempted to keep my biases in check and my mind open. I asked many questions, in no particular order. A sample:

- How do Latinos use children in low-literacy homes to interact with outside agencies?
- Are Latino communities less willing to change than others?
- How much negativity do today's immigrants experience?
- Could Latinos accept the idea of relying on neighbors?
- Are Latinos generally optimistic or pessimistic about the future?

- How quickly are people moving to smartphones and computers?
- What are the most significant **roadblocks** Latinos face?
- Do Latinos understand and value simple solutions?
- How do Latinos gauge family happiness?

I married general and specific answers to these questions with insights on issues like community development, the application of technology, human psychology, cultural nuances, and family dynamics. In combination they formed the beliefs that drive the overarching goal, strategy, and tactics outlined in this book.

Among the objectives:

- Maximize strengths at the family, neighborhood, and community levels.
- Target issues and problems that families have the potential to control.
- Understand constraints as well as needs.
- Embrace new approaches.
- Do not be afraid to advance simple ideas.
- Persuade some people, assuming that others will follow.
- Advance technology, but only if it will be used and is effective.
- Only implement ideas that are scalable.

Strategies

I have identified three strategies to reach the overarching goal of helping Latino families prepare their children for mainstream success in one generation.

- **First strategy:** Make households smarter.
- **Second strategy:** Strengthen neighborhoods and their support of the families within them.

- **Third strategy:** Advance integration of all sectors (public, private, government, and individuals) in support of families and neighborhoods.

In concert, these strategies would be geared toward strengthening Latino families in ways that advance their progress in American society. This approach recognizes that families are ultimately responsible for their own success, and that while society cannot ensure their progress, neighbors can be there to support their efforts. Finally, investment from both inside and outside Latino neighborhoods is required, and every dollar and in-kind contribution must be thoughtfully allocated and spent. Having a process to guide such support helps everyone.

In the following pages I will discuss broad approaches to achieving progress as well as specific examples of how these strategies are being used in communities across the country. The discussion is not in any way meant to be comprehensive or limiting but to show how strategic programs can potentially serve families and neighborhoods. These programs share the following qualities:

- They demonstrate how innovation can be applied to a range of issues.
- They have been shown to have a direct impact on people and communities.
- Unfortunately, they have often been underutilized.
- They often demonstrate scalability.
- They highlight the value of cooperation.
- They range from simple to complex in design.
- They use both high- and low-tech approaches.
- They have often been improved upon, shared, and used as inspiration for new and even better ideas.

Two Major Caveats

While some families with low incomes and limited education have found ways to gain substantial expertise with computers, the Internet, and other technology, many get by with just a smartphone—and others do not have even that. Everyone knows that technology has become a more and more important tool for dealing with today's problems as well as preparing for the future. For that reason, abandoning programs that help Latinos with education, health, wealth creation, and many other issues simply because they require computer access and/or expertise is impractical. Doing so would simply eliminate too many programmatic options.

In response to the technology deficit, there should be a broad-based community effort to help families purchase technology tools; teach adults how to use them; promote technology education for children and extended family members; and create neighborhood "technology mentors" who will offer support at little or no cost.

Without this approach, families and neighborhoods simply will not progress as quickly or profoundly as they need to. But if people resolve to help each other, they can overcome the gaps.

The second area where Latinos face a serious obstacle is immigration. It is an issue that has created angst and controversy for decades but that seems to have resolved itself, according to many analysts, including Jorge G. Castaneda and Douglas S. Massey. In an article in the *New York Times,* they suggest that changing human and economic dynamics have smoothed the thorny issue considerably. Their analysis: "Migration between Mexico and the United States has returned to a circular pattern where large numbers of Mexicans legally cross north to work, then return south with confidence that they can repeat the journey the next time. The reason: even as illegal Mexican migration flattened out in recent years, legal Mexican travel north rose. These migrants have their papers in order."

Why has this happened? There are many reasons, but most people agree that the major ones are the high cost of entering the United States (in terms of both money and danger); the improved Mexican economy and lower birth rates (thus a smaller potential workforce); and the decline in demand for migrant labor in the United States. Castaneda and Massey, like many other analysts, suggest that illegal immigration has now almost ceased and will remain stagnant indefinitely.

There is, of course, the continuing issue of the estimated 11.5 million undocumented residents in the United States (with an estimated 60 percent from Mexico)—many of them long-term residents. **Addressing this issue will be critical to overall success, and thankfully there now appears to be greater will to move forward than in recent years.**

For the purposes of this book, the issue at hand is the impact the range of residents in Latino neighborhoods have on the progress of those areas. As Dowell Meyers, a professor at the University of Southern California, notes, "We must shift from an immigration policy, with its emphasis on keeping newcomers out, to an immigrant policy, with an emphasis on encouraging migrants and their children to integrate into our social fabric. 'Show me your papers' should be replaced with 'Welcome to English class.'"

This is a critical point. While it is true that families can assimilate and fully and independently integrate into the larger society, neighborhoods must share a unified mindset in order to create area-wide momentum. If a neighborhood is not made up of people who think of themselves as Americans, the progress everyone wants so desperately really will not happen.

Now let us shift focus to strategies and programs that can help advance and improve families, the neighborhoods they live in, and those people interested in lending a hand in a myriad of ways.

Making Households Smarter

As the knitted doily, oddly present on the wall of my lifelong bachelor cousin, stated so eloquently, "You Can Pick Your Friends, But Not Your Relatives." My cousin always said it was a joke, but I was never really sure. And even if it was a joke, it was and is a truism.

Even in America, purported to be the world's most individualistic society, family is important. Sure, it may be a mixed blessing to many, but it does matter—and in coming years it will matter even more. Although families come in many forms, in the coming years, all American families will have more in common, particularly regarding the role of extended family. That is because the effects of the recent reset of the economy, and thus society, will not be going away for some time. As I noted earlier, the national debt, and the goal of some to extinguish overnight what is a serious but manageable long-term problem, means funding will be cut for many social programs. Public dollars will be tight, and if families hope to progress, they will need to do it pretty much on their own.

Overall people will need each other more and in different ways in this fast-paced, changing world. Younger family members may need to help older ones with language barriers. Older family members may need to help younger ones by offering college loans, planning, or guidance. Grandparents will be asked to play changing roles. Some family members will expose others to new and exciting cultural, educational, artistic, and business opportunities. Much of this additional support and guidance will happen informally, but it will all make a difference in people's lives.

Why Smarter Households Will Make Such a Difference

This strategy is founded on the obliquity idea of addressing issues indirectly. How is this approach indirect? First, it puts the responsibility and opportunity in the hands of the family—**with support from** government, community-based organizations, or any other entity. Second, it empowers the family to set priorities and allocate their time and resources accordingly. Third, it asks families to be more proactive: to prevent problems from occurring and to look at the whole of the family.

Overall, any family gains an advantage when it is smarter. Smart families know how to prevent problems in the first place, and they know how to advance their own best interest in innumerable ways. In addition, these families are able to blend foresight and flexibility: they look ahead, have a general plan for their future, and monitor things well enough to make adjustments when unforeseen circumstances occur.

Undoubtedly it will be difficult for many families to attain such high-level abilities, but never sell people short. These skills are necessary in today's world where complexity challenges all people to find the best answers for themselves, protect their short- and long-term interests, and establish a level of independence while also leading their neighborhoods, joining broader society in every way, and establishing an ambitious future vision for themselves.

Finally, and probably most importantly, making families smarter helps them strengthen the protective factors that increase families' well-being and the safety of their children—a link supported by research, according to Magnolia Place in Los Angeles, a national model for community strengthening. With support, families can learn how to nurture their children; become healthier and more economically secure; create social connections with family and friends; enhance their individual resilience by practicing courage and flexibility; help their children develop socially and emotionally by encouraging communication and supporting their eagerness to learn; and gain concrete support from friends and community.

We will discuss how to strengthen families by breaking the subject down into three areas: major initiatives, educational support, and building self-esteem.

Major Initiatives

Flow of Information: "If Information Isn't Power, It's the Way to Gain It"

Regardless of social status, there probably is no family in America that would disagree that family life is complex and stressful. Some people are fortunate to have the financial means and contacts to move through life with less strain, but that is generally not true of most families. Whether it is navigating the school or health-care system; developing formal banking relationships; working through apartment rental agreements; selecting college savings plans; navigating county or state agencies to find help for a disabled child; dealing with an unscrupulous car dealer; settling a lawsuit ...the challenges are almost unlimited.

If families cannot access critical information when they need it, they cannot function in this society. They cannot normalize their daily lives, which would free them to contemplate a brighter future for their children and themselves. Earlier in the book I outlined the everyday challenges faced by low-income families and the decision fatigue they endure as they constantly juggle purchasing and other decisions in light of a pocketbook that is usually much too small. So, whenever possible, it is critical to give them information and access to resources that will reduce this kind of cognitive stress.

The irony is this kind of information already exists in many forms—and, in a way, that is the problem. In today's world there is simply too much information. The world is drowning in it. Add to this scenario many Latinos' limited English literacy and, for some, a lack of information-processing skills, and the challenge is formidable.

How can we approach this need from the Latino users' point of view? We should start with five critical questions: 1) What do they know? 2) What do they need or want to know? 3) What form should the information take? 4) What distribution system would they prefer today and over time? 5) What approach would help develop their information-processing skills?

Let's address these questions one at a time.

What do they know? The Latino family knowledge base is as varied as the families themselves. A few key variables—country of origin, extended family network, education levels, and overall support structure—dictate most of the answer.

What do they need or want to know? That question may be easiest to answer. The most critical issues would undoubtedly revolve around health and health services, primary and secondary education, finances, and available government services. Many households would also benefit from understanding how the broader societal system works (a macro view). In some cases, Latinos need more than simple information: they need someone to help frame a complex issue or problem, so they can better understand its true ramifications and consequences. This can be a complex job, or it can be as simple as outlining three points that cover the vast majority of what they need to know.

What form should the information take? How the information is packaged—e.g., Q & As, a conversational discussion, extended or abbreviated text, light or heavy graphics—will depend to a great degree on the medium. Overall, the broadest range of distribution is desirable as it presents the best opportunity to reach people at different times and through different media: audio, visual, and print. However, every communication should carry a consistent set of messages on how Latinos can find more information on their own, either online or through more traditional methods.

To make this complex effort successful, a host of experts should be involved, including social scientists, subject experts, media, and advertising agencies, along with local community-based organizations who might precede this effort with their own approaches to break the ice. Additionally, people need to do everything possible to support the existing information lines and other such programs that are already serving communities across the nation.

English is Fundamental to Progress in This Country. Period.

Research has confirmed for some time that every generation of Latinos embraces the English language, but adults need to accelerate the transition to English and overall literacy rates since adult literacy is essential to children's educational development. A 2010 news release from the National Institutes of Health noted that building parents' literacy skills may be the best way to boost their children's achievement. According to the NIH, a mother's reading skill is the greatest determinant of her children's future academic success, even outweighing other factors such as neighborhood and family income. **Parents who learn to read in Spanish in preparation for English and read to their children become powerful role models and are more likely to interact with their children's schools.**

Many volunteers have taught Latinos literacy skills one-on-one or in small classes, but it is clear that with the scale of the literacy problem Latinos will have to embrace technology through the use of computers and even smartphones. The current goals should be to find the best teaching software at the best possible price and to find ways to mentor adults who are trying to gain Spanish literacy and then move them to English.

There are a few prototype literacy programs already in place around the country, including Centro Latino for Literacy (CLL), a Los Angeles-based nonprofit dedicated to teaching Spanish-dominant Latinos how to read in Spanish and then transfer to English. CLL was founded in 1991 to address the pressing need for basic literacy instruction among immigrant Latinos. Then, as now, most non-literate Spanish speakers would enroll in English as a Second Language (ESL) programs, find them too difficult, and after struggling to keep up without success, drop out. CLL reversed this process by teaching students *first* to read and write in Spanish. This approach builds the students' foundational skills—and their confidence—so they are able not only to learn English, but also to increase their employment prospects and economic situation, support their children's education, and pursue their dreams and aspirations.

Centro Latino builds Spanish literacy through two programs:

- Leamos ("Let's Read") is a self-paced, web-based curriculum to teach basic reading and writing skills to Spanish speakers. An indirect benefit is that students also become comfortable around computers. For many, it is their first exposure to this technology, and they overcome their fear of it in the process of learning to read and write.
- Listos ("We're Ready") engages students to use their newly acquired literacy to learn functional life skills, such as basic math, grammar, financial literacy, and health literacy as well as ESL and computer skills offered by partner programs.

Significantly increasing Latino literacy will require a neighborhood-wide effort. Fortunately, the cost of software is shrinking and access to computers is growing. Finding tutors to help individuals and groups will be the major challenge.

College Gap Widening
Longitudinal Educ. Attainment: % of Some College degree and over

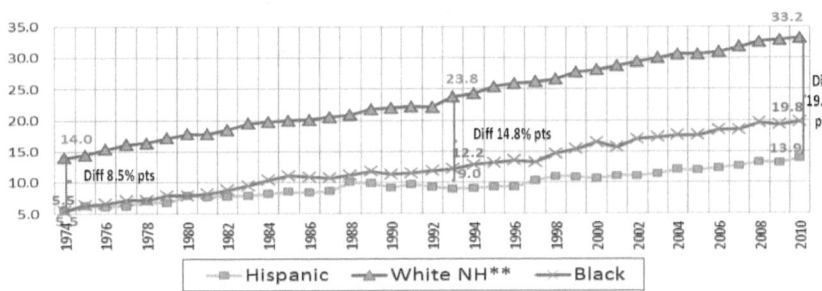

- The % of Hispanics attaining some level of college degree has nearly doubled over the last 4 decades, from around 5.5% to 9.3%
- Yet, Hispanic college level attainment gap vs. WNH has doubled over last 4 decades from 8.5% to 19.3%
- While, African American was 60% below White NH in 1974, their attainment has improved to 40% below White NH, while Hispanics have made minimal gains during the same time period.

Source: 1947-2010 Current Population Survey

Of US Hispanics aged 5 to 17, 15.5 percent reside in households that do not speak English very well.

Advancing Latino Children

In "Kids First: Five Big Ideas for Transforming Children's Live and America's Future," David L. Kirp makes these recommendations:

- Provide more support to new parents.
- Offer high-quality early education.
- Link schools and communities to what both can offer children.
- Give all youngsters access to a caring, stable adult mentor.
- Provide a nest egg to help pay for college or kick-start a career.

It is clear that caring for children should be a community- and neighborhood-wide effort—which is the focus of the next chapter.

Keeping Families Together

According to Kay S. Hymowitz, author of *Marriage and Caste in America*, single-motherhood has been an economic catastrophe for women. Poverty remains relatively rare among married couples with children: the US Census Bureau puts only 8.8 percent in that category, up from 6.7 percent since the start of the Great Recession. But more than 40 percent of single-mother families are poor, up from 37 percent before the downturn.

Figures for Latino families are more difficult to acquire, but if the numbers are anywhere close to the total figure for American women, this is significant and suggests there is a role for **extended families, premarital counseling, and contraception options.**

Among all American ethnic groups, Hispanics are the least likely to have health insurance, with approximately 43 percent of Hispanics aged eighteen to sixty-four uninsured. This is due to the fact that many workers have multiple-part-time jobs and/or work for smaller companies that do not offer insurance

Rethinking the American Dream

Throughout this book I have listed a number of ways in which the world is changing. Add to that list the changing idea of ownership as the strategy for and ultimately the symbol of prosperity. *Renting* may be the key word going forward.

In a thoughtful and convincing article adapted from his book *Better, Stronger, Faster: The Myth of the American Decline and the Rise of a New Economy*, Daniel Gross outlines the concept of "renting prosperity" and its value to many Americans. This concept is important for Latinos to understand because it offers an approach that could be of great long-term value to thousands, if not millions, of families striving to move up the economic ladder.

While acknowledging that there has historically been a bias against the concept of renting a dwelling, Gross argues that it is now a viable option for many people. After all, the typical consumer spends 32 percent of his or her income on shelter, and people have borrowed and accelerated their debt in order to manage. In today's world that is not a good thing. And there are other reasons to avoid buying a home besides the up-front costs. There are high maintenance costs, particularly in older neighborhoods; a lack of home appreciation in many cases; and reduced mobility in an era when flexibility to move for a job opportunity is critical. Although there is evidence that for some families buying is still smart, the issue is not as clear-cut as it once was. In late 2011, it was cheaper to rent than to own in 72 percent of American metropolitan areas, and that number may be increasing as construction of rental units is outpacing that of single-family dwellings.

Although housing is a family's most significant expenditure, transportation costs account for 16 percent of household spending, or approximately $8,588 a year for the average driver. Now there are Zipcar and a few other alternatives to vehicle ownership that can save families thousands of dollars a year. This is all just the start of a renting trend that includes clothes, college textbooks, rooms in private homes, and even jewelry. Not all renting options are for everyone, but they do demonstrate that the economy is changing and that families should keep up with the new options available to them.

Maybe It's Time to Rethink the Extended Family

Observers have noted for some time that Latinos are family oriented, a trait that often reaches beyond the traditional nuclear family. But are Latinos maximizing this dynamic to its full extent? There are many Latino grandparents taking care of grandchildren, but in these harsh economic times, and with some of the economic challenges likely to continue for years, there is no such thing as too much family support. It is ironic that some wealthy families pool their money for investing; bring nephews, nieces, and cousins into the family business; and find other ways to offer support, thus enhancing the family's collective future prosperity. Latinos would be smart to follow that model and consider stronger connections with extended relatives.

Earlier, I described the need for Latinos to rededicate themselves and their families to a plan that offers greater self-sufficiency going forward. This could include elements like increased savings, cautious investing, careful consideration of buying versus renting, and similar financial strategies. This recommendation assumes that all Americans may be receiving less aid from the government than they have received in the past.

Beyond Family

As more Latinos move in search of work and other opportunities, direct family support may decline, and in that case "family mentors" would be hugely important. Latinos with a little (or a lot) more experience could counsel young families as they try to weave their way through a complicated world of budgeting, schools, health care, and so much more. Some mentors could also fill in as part-time babysitters, a critical need that often hampers women in search of full- or part-time work. Religious institutions and community-based organizations may be able to extend their involvement in this area.

Education: The Great Equalizer

To allow education to become the great equalizer "Children's reading scores improve dramatically when their parents are involved in helping them learn to read," according to the National Center for Family Literacy. This reinforces that idea that education begins at home, and while Latinos should expect a great deal from schools, they should demand more from families.

There are not enough "learning households."

Successful education depends on the student, the school, the teacher, the parents, and the student's friends. (I have probably left someone out, but these five factors are a good start.) The major point is that it is not just the school or the teacher that determines whether a child succeeds or fails academically; everyone has to contribute, regardless of background. So, I am proposing some ideas that cost little but can have a significant impact on children's future. In fact, their collective importance cannot be stressed enough. Some proposals are based on science, while a few are chicken-soup-type bromides. Every culture has those.

As you consider these ideas, keep in mind the point made by Malcolm Gladwell in his book *Outliers*: wealthier kids are not smarter than poor kids—they outlearn them. They get more educational stimuli at school, after school, at home, on weekends, and all summer. Latino kids need the same advantages.

Also keep this in mind: a 2009 national survey of Latinos aged sixteen to twenty-five who do not have a high school degree, who are not enrolled in high school, and who have no plans to enroll reported that the main reason was the need to "support the family."

Talk, Talk, Talk and Question

Talking is power. Researchers have shown that a child in a home with a highly educated family will hear five million more words by the time he or she enters kindergarten than a child from a less-educated home. This matters because little kids have minds like sponges: they learn from every word, every new word and every question posed to them, and from the basic interaction that is conversation. If Latino parents, regardless of education, simply talked to their children from the time they were born, those children would enter school better prepared, and the positive repercussions might extend throughout their schooling because it is foundational. The cost is zero; the impact is profound.

Question, Question, Question

Historically, Latino families value respect for elders and sometimes questions are frowned upon. To the extent this still exists, it has to change. Children's curiosity is a wonderful thing, and it should be encouraged at every age.

Reading Counts

The companion activity is reading, and Americans as a whole—and Latinos in particular—have serious literacy issues. Any effort in this area is good for everyone. If Latino parents have to struggle to read a children's book in English or Spanish, they should hand the task of reading aloud to a sibling or friend. It is worth the effort. The child learns from the process and gains an understanding that books are good things to be appreciated. **Children emulate adults. Parents need to be seen reading, going to the library and buying books.**

Books Make a Statement

An interesting study found that when junior high students selected twelve books and were asked to place them on living room shelves over the summer, three important things happened: First, they read them. Second, they returned to school in the fall better prepared. Third, and most important, the household was enriched because it acquired a "learning household" status. For some families, that might seem only slightly important, but for many households it was a dramatic improvement. **As a follow-up, parents should provide an allowance so children can buy books.**

Rachel Moya's Approach

Here's the chicken soup: Though my mother was a high school dropout, she told me from the time I could understand words that I was going to college.

I believed her.

Every Child Can Benefit from Personal Help after School

Even though household budgets are tight, Latino parents should consider paying older youth to be tutors, if only at a nominal rate. This would send a message to younger kids that neighborhood kids, who are often the kids they look up to, are smart, and that education is cool. This also enhances the self-esteem of the older youth.

Growing College Enrollment

Table 3.1 College Enrollment of 18- to 24-Year-Olds, 2010-2011 (in thousands)

	2010	2011	Change	Percentage Change
All	12,213	12,570	357	3%
Hispanic	1,814	2,079	265	15%
White	7,663	7,882	219	3%
Black	1,692	1,639	-53	-3%
Asian	811	748	-63	-8%

Notes: "White" includes only non-Hispanic whites. The figures above refer to the white-, black- and Asian-alone populations. College enrollment refers to persons enrolled in a two-year college or a four-year college or university. It also includes those enrolled at private and public colleges and universities.

Source: Pew Hispanic Center analysis of the October 2010 and 2011 Current Population Surveys

Latino Grandparents often Wear Multiple Hats

As with the African-American community, Latino grandparents often play a more significant role in the lives of their grandchildren than do grandparents in the general population. Whether because of broken homes, absent fathers, or parents working multiple jobs or longer hours, Latino grandparents take on more responsibilities and an expanded role. Add to this the fact that they often live near or even with their children and their hours with the grandchildren and influence over their lives take on added dimensions. For this reason it would be smart for schools and community groups to factor this reality into their outreach and for organizations, such as the AARP, to offer more information about child development in today's world. Such outreach would be important to the children and valuable to the grandparents and parents.

Kids As the Household "Voice"

Until everyone in the household is literate, Latino children will continue to play a unique role in American society as the ears and voice for many households. This has long been a reality, especially for households with foreign-born parents but US-born children. Children, and particularly teens, have been their families' readers, translators, and even decision makers, predominantly in consumer purchasing and in interaction with government agencies like the DMV. While this is an unusual role for young people, it is not altogether unheard of among other populations though not to the same extent. Marketers have long known that teens and older children are often more knowledgeable than their parents about products like home electronics, computers, and even cars. The unique role of Latino children as "language filterers" was effectively maximized recently when the US Census Bureau engaged children to help their parents with limited reading skills. Schools need to incorporate the role of these kids into outreach efforts.

Parent-Teacher Meetings Shouldn't Be Avoided

A final but important note: parental interaction with teachers is critical to supporting children's education, but many parents with little education or English-speaking skills are too intimidated to attend parent-teacher meetings. While their fear may be understandable, they must overcome it; in fact, they must recognize that teachers are eager for this kind of interaction. If language is a problem, parents can bring along an older sibling, a neighbor, a friend, or another family member. Maybe the best approach would be to arrange for a group "parents-teacher" meeting that might include several parents with children in the same class. Though the discussion would be less student-specific, parents (and the teacher) could learn a great deal, and over time this could lead to individual meetings. **Similarly, schools should find volunteer opportunities since children do better when parents are involved in their school.**

The examples in this education section often build on the idea outlined in an earlier section of this book—that is, doing what works. While no single solution will solve every education challenge, when implemented in concert, these relatively easy and inexpensive strategies can give Latino kids the foundation to excel.

As I suggested, there are also higher-level online programs that more Latino families should take advantage of, either individually, in groups, or through schools. Here is a sampling, ranging from programs that are fun and make learning more enjoyable, to those that help students overcome obstacles, to those that are quite challenging and help develop big-picture thinking:

Reading Eggs

This program introduces reading to very young children and enables foreign-born parents to link their reading progress and English pronunciation with their child's. Reading Eggs engages children with interactive animation, games, songs, and testing. It focuses on a core reading curriculum based on the most up-to-date research on how children learn to read.

Website: ReadingEggs.com

iMentor

This program serves as a medium through which low-income high school students are mentored and tutored by professionals from local small- and medium-sized businesses. Communicating primarily by e-mail, mentors educate students about the leadership and professional skills they will need in order to be successful in the business world. The emphasis on communicating via technology makes this program very cost-effective.

Project K-Nect

Through this initiative teachers assign problems to students, students get support from their peers, and the results can be forwarded to the parents, all through the use of smartphones. The use of smartphones as an educational tool allows for greater communication between teacher and student and between student and peer/mentor, and it lets parents closely monitor their child's progress. Currently, the major cost of the program is that of providing smartphones to students.

Crear Futuros

This program offers both academic and family support to selected high-risk community college students. The peer-to-peer component assigns a mentor in a four-year college who has had experiences similar to those of the mentee and his or her family. Sega's Manaba software helps track the mentee's academic progress; gauge points of risk (absences, grades); and monitor his or her emotional responses to the college experience, which are a critical factor in success in higher education. The mentorship/support is offered via the Sega gaming platform.

Scratch

This computer literacy program is particularly popular among twelve- and thirteen-year-olds. It offers a fun, simple environment for learning a computer language, enabling young beginners to get results without having to learn syntactically correct writing first. It is intended to motivate further learning by letting users playfully experiment and create projects. More than six hundred thousand people have Scratch accounts.

AT&T Mobile Apps

This is part of a $250 million campaign to help more students graduate from college and make the country more globally competitive. It uses focused technology to connect with students in new and more effective ways, such as with interactive games, Web-based content, and social media. The program also enables students in underserved communities to explore careers through internships in areas related to twenty-first-century skills.

Apple in Education

Here is just a partial list from Apple's exciting portfolio of educational programs:

- Grammar In HD: Improves grammar and vocabulary with a multiple-choice quiz system featuring more than eighteen hundred questions in twenty categories.
- Mathboard: Offers customized arithmetic drills, quizzes, and more for kids from kindergarten through elementary school.
- Wolfram Algebra Course Assist: Explains and helps students solve specific algebra problems with step-by-step instructions.
- StarWalk: Shows placement of stars, constellations, and satellites in real time.

MyMoney.gov

This website is designed to educate youth, teachers, parents, employers, military veterans, retirees, and researchers about proper money management. Using the resources of the US government, this free online platform compiles information from twenty-two federal organizations in one simple site. All resources are web-based, and downloadable documents are in English and Spanish. This website has been publicized as one of the top ten online financial literacy resources.

Website: MyMoney.gov

Jump$tart

This program is offered by a coalition of national organizations seeking to advance the financial literacy of students from pre-kindergarten through college. It is continuously updated based on the latest research, new advancements, and the evolution of markets.

Jump$tart provides youth with lifelong financial decision-making skills, and it offers innovative resources for financial advocacy, research, and education. The program allows parents look up and learn about financial resources in four different languages, and it adapts to the progress of the individual student.

Jump$tart is funded by more than 150 corporate, academic, nonprofit, and government organizations, and it includes a network of forty-nine affiliated state coalitions that operate on a local level to promote financial literacy. This program is free to the public.

Website: JumpStart.org

College Match

According to a recent Century Foundation report, the most underrepresented group of Americans at the nation's top colleges and universities are students from low-income families. This is due in part to the fact that most high school counselors are overwhelmed, and most parents cannot afford personal college counselors, SAT preparatory courses, essay consultants, extensive college visits, and other forms of help that more affluent college applicants enjoy.

College Match tries to bridge that gap by identifying low-income high school sophomores with strong academic records and providing them with intensive, individualized services comparable to those affluent students often receive. Those include SAT prep classes; assistance filling out college application forms; financial assistance for college visits; contacting college admission offices as advocates; and negotiating on behalf of students for more grant assistance.

The difference between this program and others is the focus on high academic achievers and elite colleges and much more intensive one-on-one services.

Becoming Smarter and Prouder and Controlling Our Destiny

There has always been great pride among Latinos. But there has also been doubt, often imposed by the broader society upon what is a relatively new and unique population. Regardless of the reasons, this situation has to change, and Latinos must lead the way in controlling their own societal role, self-image, public image, and future. Here are some ways to do that:

Make Goals and Plans

It has been proven: young people in junior and senior high school who have plans for the future and articulate them—even if they are fuzzy—do better in the long run. Students should think of a goal as an end point (e.g., becoming a rocket scientist) and then plan a strategy for getting there: first, enroll at a community college to save money; second, attend a major research university to study aeronautical engineering; third, land a job at Boeing.

Ask, "How was your day?"

Research shows that just asking this question improves your child's attitude, and that is good.

Visit Museums

Families that visit art museums are accomplishing many things simultaneously. They are not only enjoying time together, but also, for many Latino families, they are breaking the perceived barrier between themselves and the rest of society. They are welcomed and they belong. They are also advancing their children's education and learning through art. Through art education and exposure, children enhance important cognitive skills, including evaluation, integration, reasoning, recognizing multiple solutions, collaborative problem solving, and creative thinking.

Eliminate Fear of Failure and Encourage Children to Take Risk

According to Professor David Kirp, although many young people lack self-confidence, minority students are especially prone to the fear of failure. This fear, which psychologists label "stereotype vulnerability," can start at a very early age and undermine academic performance. The student does poorly, his or her fears are confirmed, and the cycle repeats itself.

This is a longstanding problem that I believe will only disappear through concerted efforts by parents, family, teachers, administrators, and all those in contact with young people. Here are three places parents can start: (1) They should demonstrate the pride and confidence they want their children to embrace; (2) They should take every opportunity to tell their children how important and unique they are; (3) Every day, when their children return from school, they should ask them, "How was your day?"—because as I previously noted, research has shown that children respond to and value that simple question.

Gather a Posse

Many believe that to succeed in a competitive world younger workers need a network of supporters (a "posse") and creative people who will give them ideas to think about and perhaps use. Maybe everyone needs a posse.

Think and Act with the Future in Mind

Social scientists know that humans are frivolous about the future. Behavioral economist David Laibson notes, "There is a fundamental tension, in humans and other animals, between seizing available rewards in the present, and being patient for rewards in the future. People want instant gratification now and to be patient in the future."

This is fundamental and critical given that all people are going to have to say no to consumer items today so that they can pay for housing, education, and health and retirement costs tomorrow. This is a fact people are aware of, yet most are unable to act rationally when faced with tough economic choices. Everyone would benefit by making progress in this area.

The Power to Learn Confidence

In *Outliers*, his groundbreaking book on how people achieve success, Malcolm Gladwell offers a range of insights, including the value of timing—that is, when immigrants arrived in the United States and with what skills. As I noted at the beginning of this book, most immigrant Latinos arrived in the United States after the knowledge economy had begun to take hold, and few had the personal background or skill set necessary to succeed post-1973. As a result they've attempted to progress the old-fashioned way, through hard work. And while many Latino families have passed along this most critical of attributes to their children, they have lagged behind in other areas, negatively affecting their socioeconomic status.

Without specifying any particular population, Gladwell reinforces what is seen in families. Generally, prosperous people often feel entitled and wield power when necessary, particularly when it comes to advancing their children. Middle-class families interact with their children, demonstrate "concerted cultivation," and challenge them to stand up for themselves in every situation. Poorer people follow a "natural growth mode" and too often fail to cultivate their children's skills and interests. They are often intimidated by other people and by institutions such as schools—a fact that hurts their children's chances for success.

This does not have to be. There are many examples of low-income, less-educated Latinos who have broken the mold. I will cite one example that has inspired many:

Maria Elena Perez and her husband, Samuel Sr., were immigrants from Mexico. Neither advanced beyond the sixth grade. Yet every one of their eleven children graduated from college—six from the University of Southern California, a prestigious private university.

To support the family and the children's educational pursuits, Mr. Perez held three jobs. He would have dinner in the mid-afternoon with his children after a full day at a machine shop, and then he would head off to his second job, on the assembly line at a General Motors plant. On weekends, he earned extra money as a gardener. Mrs. Perez was a tireless volunteer at the children's school.

My assumption is that Mr. and Mrs. Perez were often uncomfortable and maybe at times overwhelmed, but they overcame their hindrances to support their children's education. They are heroes and can be emulated.

Is there one solution for all families? Of course not. Are there combinations of actions that can help many families? Yes. But what's important to keep in mind is the overall direction being advanced here. People live in homes and apartments, but they also live in neighborhoods. It is time to maximize the collective strength of the people who make neighborhoods vibrant, or potentially so. That is where we turn next.

Strengthening Latino Neighborhoods

In the past, neighborhoods had a sense of community, and while it is possible that this is an idealized past, there should be a return to that community feeling. Today this could be called a social network.

In his new book, *Stealth of Nations: The Global Rise of the Informal Economy*, Robert Neuwirth points out that informal economies account for trillions of dollars in commerce and employ half of all workers worldwide. He notes that these enterprises are critical sources of entrepreneurialism, innovation, and self-reliance, and they have improved the lives of millions. Neuwirth says this "self-reliance economy" is growing across the globe and by 2020 will employ two-thirds of all workers. In many cases these entrepreneurs work independently, but they also have relationships with global brands like Procter & Gamble and many others. Because they tend to be small, they can make quick adjustments to respond to consumers' needs, often giving insight to larger companies that usually, but not always, make the products.

I'm not suggesting that America's inner-city neighborhoods mirror third-world regions, but just as governments, corporations, and opinion makers must understand the new self-reliance economy, people must begin to realign thinking when it comes to Latino neighborhoods in this country.

Although there is economic opportunity in these neighborhoods, there is far more potential in cooperative efforts that benefit children, adults, and entire households. In this section I will explore new ways to think about neighborhoods; how to improve the collective thinking in these areas; and how to maximize their potential and make them part of the solution for Latino families striving to improve their lives.

Why Neighborhoods?

In the post-World War II years, the American way was to find a nice, affordable house with a yard in a good neighborhood with good schools. If it was close to shopping and maybe church, that was a bonus. If the neighbors were friendly, that was another bonus. As the years went on, Americans, considered the most individualistic people in the world, stayed with that pattern—although some would argue that it changed as many people did not even know their closest neighbors.

Back to the need to look at neighborhoods—and Latino neighborhoods, in particular—differently:

As I outlined previously, for a variety of historical, timing, cultural, and economic reasons, Latinos have found themselves in the precarious position of trying to catch up with others in American society in a slow-growth era when the national and global economies are fundamentally changing and the government at all levels is tightening its belt. So to whom can Latinos turn for help? Should they look to Washington, their State capital, or their city or county government, or, as I have often discussed to their own "community"? My contention is that the broader Latino community is worth holding on to, but the better answer is to come closer and reconnect with neighborhood in a fundamentally different way.

In today's and tomorrow's neighborhoods, residents' attitudes toward it must change from "When can I leave and where can I go?" to "How can we all help make it better, and what can we collectively receive that helps our families in the process?" A significant contributor will be learning to use the newest technology available to advance a modern neighborhood social network. A 2011 Pew Research Center report noted that Internet users, especially social media users, are more likely than non-users to be active in volunteer groups and other such organizations.

Yet face-to-face interaction will be critical as well—a neighborhood cannot succeed collectively without it. This is social networking not for fun, but to truly advance people. It requires broadband *and* feet.

There will be others, but two much-debated cultural characteristics will quickly rise to the surface as key factors in this strategy: individualism and self-reliance. Earlier in the book I explained the perspective that Latinos are somewhat individualistic (do not often join organizations) and avoid the collective (except for family). My hope is that the seriousness of Latinos' current situation, the complex problems they face, and the challenge of meeting the one-generation goal will sway them at least to accept, if not embrace, the need for collective effort. There is also the issue of trust, although *reliance* may be a better concept. Trusting someone puts most people in a vulnerable or even defensive position. Relying on someone is different. For example, if I provide your business with raw materials to manufacture a product, you must rely on the quality of what I deliver or risk producing potentially substandard goods. Thus, you have an incentive to pay a fair rate for my quality materials. Conversely, I have the incentive to provide quality raw materials so that you will continue to prosper. I must rely on your continued success so I have a place to sell my goods.

In the same way, families trying to move up the socioeconomic ladder can clearly gain from the expertise of and simple help from others like themselves. Then, they in turn can help others through their unique abilities. Reciprocity can be a wonderful thing, particularly for people with limited resources and education. It can be pure win-win.

How to Improve Neighborhood Collective Thinking

Large organizations in all sectors have found it increasingly difficult to improve and prosper independently. The world is too complex, the competition is too high, and the need to respond quickly to consumers or constituents makes it impossible to have all the needed skills under one roof. The same is true of individuals and families. To improve their lives they need the help of others, who they must help in return. There is clear evidence that modern society is returning to past eras with its focus on community support, *even though in some cases the new supporters may be across the globe.* A growing willingness to share everything—from a spare room to a car to clothes—is partial evidence.

Electronic social networks contain information, entertain, provide educational resources about political and social issues, help people band together to take on companies and institutions more powerful than any individual, and even offer up potential spouses. Though social networking has a growing place in contemporary life, many believe it cannot totally replace direct human interaction (although a few individuals are pressing this point). I believe this is particularly true in the case of Latino neighborhoods, because while neighbors' language, ethnicity, nation of origin, and other socioeconomic characteristics might not be exactly the same, there are also great similarities that make for potentially deep connections within crowds. When you consider that people in Latino neighborhoods often have limited education and little time, the concept of "crowds" is invaluable and may very well help shape the future for many Latinos.

The essence of the crowd concept is captured in the cover of James Surowiecki's 2004 book, *The Wisdom of Crowds: Why the Many Are Smarter than the Few and How the Collective Wisdom Shapes Business, Economics, Societies and Nations.* The author points out that groups and group thinking generate answers for frivolous issues, like helping fair-goers guess the weight of a bull or a studio audience supporting a contestant on a game show, as well as important ones such as finding the location of a sunken submarine or, on a macro level, speculating the direction of global markets. All this suggests that across the board it is easier to make groups smarter than individuals. A key challenge is to give the group process the chance to succeed by including a diversity of perspectives, allowing everyone equal time, avoiding domination by any individual, and banning any form of intimidation.

According to another influential book, *Crowdsourcing*, the power of the many can be leveraged to accomplish feats that were once the province of the specialized few. Whether it is tens of thousands of bird watchers helping a university department categorize birds, or amateur photographers around the world contributing photos to iStock, or contributions to Wikipedia, the idea is the same.

Through Crowdsourcing, things are accomplished that otherwise could not be achieved by individuals. It is rooted in a fundamentally egalitarian principle: every individual possesses some knowledge or talent that some other individual will find valuable. But ultimately it comes down to collective intelligence. If you ask twenty thousand engineers to help solve a problem, you will get the solution—not because one person had it, but because a combination of smaller, key insights will lead to something greater.

The likeliest supporters of these concepts are young people, who make up a vast portion of Latinos in any neighborhood. Their understanding of technology, diverse cultural groups, and the array of cutting-edge ideas they see in play all around them has not been maximized. Whether it is the wisdom of crowds played out around a neighbor's kitchen table, or thousands of Latinos across the country offering their thoughts on a problem plaguing Latino families, the impact of these new approaches could be extraordinary. If Latinos do not begin to tap their collective brainpower, they will squander an unbelievably potent tool.

There are also new ways in which both traditional and new thinking can make an impact in today's world. Take the power of networks, word-of-mouth and "influentials". Small and large networks of friends, contacts, and even friends of friends are still valuable in today's society. As any marketer, politician, or business owner will acknowledge, people learn about products, services, job opportunities, and just about everything else by word of mouth. Finally, "influentials" carry that tag for a reason: they often are tuned in to the pulse of a neighborhood because they are good at collecting information, synthesizing it, and making the connections others cannot (and often do not even see). They also have time for almost anyone because that is how they learn and transfer their currency of information and influence.

While the neighborhood and its influentials should be a critical base for Latinos, it is also important to understand the "weak ties" idea because it increasingly comes into play. Here's the concept: while it is important to build a cadre of close friends and contacts, branching out is still necessary. Job hunting is an obvious example. If you limit your search to jobs that friends are aware of, your world will by definition be small, mostly because there will be duplication. Your friends know many of the same people and will gather the same information. But if you branch out to different people, or weak ties, your world becomes larger. This example has very real implications given that the average job tenure in the United States is 4.4 years, and most people will have eleven different jobs in their lifetime.

Neighborhoods Plans as Part of the Broader Solution

Advancing and reenergizing Latino dominated neighborhoods across the country can be done, and the benefit to families would be profound. Because they are all different, there is not set process, but there are three common areas: leadership and support; a critical assessment of the area; and a plan.

Leadership can literally come from anyone with the desire, commitment, and vision to see change happen. They can be young or old; educated or not; with or without means; experienced or novice. The greatest attribute is desire to make things better.

To make this happen Latinos need to encourage, train, and support not just dynamic people with credentials, but those with less experience but who have common sense, insights, an ability to motivate others and a true commitment to an area.

While leaders are critical, they cannot do things alone. They must become adept at attracting workers and supporters in part by using the skills, techniques, and assets reviewed earlier, such as "the wisdom of crowds," "crowdsourcing," and "influentials."

An assessment of the area can have many facets, but identifying strengths may be most important because the process can offer cause for greater optimism than might initially be seen. Here are examples:

The power of history. If the neighborhood is downtrodden, but there is an historical attachment to the area, there is the potential to build on that past. Latinos seem to have a strong sense of place: there is a culture built into the fabric of the buildings, parks, roads, and places where people congregate.

The value of families. Over the years families have been the foundation for an area and continue to be the drivers of improvement. Families continue to have influence, but sometimes they simply need new and probably younger blood to lend a hand.

The value of institutions. An institution can also be a catalyst for improvement. A college or university, a hospital, or a major business can be of huge value. Sometimes new management simply needs a push and an assurance that the neighborhood is interested and willing to roll up its sleeves.

Expanded female leadership. Latinas have always played a pivotal role in community development, but their strength is clearly on the rise as they build knowledge and skills in America's college and universities. Like all women, they have proven they have the emotional intelligence that is a major asset in the changing economy.

Shared identity may be the strongest attribute that can drive real progress at the neighborhood level, particularly if the sense of connectedness lies within a broader context as outlined in this book.

A Plan

- The catalyst for the initial plan would come ideally from a "leader" or a group with the attributes previously outlined, but they could literally come from anywhere. It could be two neighbors; people associated with an established institution like a church; a community-based organization; a local elected official; a neighborhood business; or an interested school principal. The key is to get started.
- **The plan can be formal, but it need not be. Just a few small projects to improve the neighborhood, such as a critically**

needed cross-walk at a dangerous intersection, a neighborhood literacy program, extending the hours at the local library, or placing pressure on a local store to improve the quality of its fruit and vegetables can be a catalyst. The needs are unique to every neighborhood.

- In addition to finding a few specific solutions for the neighborhood, people would be building a real community and finding their voices, thus attracting attention and recognition from elected officials and other decision makers and influential people.

- Over time local leaders should design formal, customized plans that meet the needs of their unique areas. At the same time they will need to educate neighborhood residents on programs, both public and private, that already exist. Many of these efforts are technologically based and offer unique solutions that families should take full advantage of. The following sections describe many of these programs along with additional unique approaches for neighborhood improvement.

New Ways to Support Neighborhoods Already Exist

A critical opportunity for Latino engagement is the informal economy in which they procure work, purchase products and services, and in general advance their day-to-day living through other individuals rather than formal businesses. It is an example of Latino adaptation, resilience, and inventiveness with an entrepreneurial spirit. It takes place every day through informal networks and word of mouth, which are generally effective but often too time-intensive. To speed up the process and save people time, I recommend the development of local, centralized networks of online communities, or electronic phone apps that could connect neighbors. People could use the apps to barter, sell products or services, and arrange for family needs (such as having another parent pick up a child from school). Because the network would be entirely local, users would save the time and money required to interact with someone across town.

There already are a range of apps for the vast majority of people who have mobile phones or at the very least texting capability. **Yardsale** lets people browse through items for sale based on the proximity of the seller. **Highligh**t links people in close proximity who may have something to sell or share. **Bondy** is building a virtual marketplace over an existing social network, and **Ketup** shows a photo feed of nearby items that are for sale. This area is expanding quickly and will only strengthen the working of the informal economy for everyone.

The app-driven informal economy advances the obliquity idea because as locals interacting with one another on issues of commerce, they are more inclined to engage discussions about their shared community and ways to improve it. This would not be the first reason to design such a system, but the indirect benefits could be great.

Taking Neighborhood Action to the Next Level

In an ideal world, every community would be connected to a Magnolia Place Community Initiative. This far-reaching effort began with a question: What would it take to enable thirty-five thousand children living within five square miles of the Magnolia Catchment Area in Los Angeles to break all records of success in their education and their health and in the quality of the nurturing care and economic stability they receive from their families and community?

That question is the driving force behind the Magnolia Place Community Initiative where more than seventy county, city, and community programs have united to make this dream a reality. The founders recognized that it requires a different commitment from individuals and organizations to create the environment necessary to continuously improve, align, and coordinate efforts to achieve and sustain community health and well-being.

Magnolia Place has effectively integrated the efforts of nonprofits as well as the public and private sectors to support families and children. Programs are mostly focused on adoption and foster care service; education, health, and recreation; mental health; parenting; and an array of other critically need services.

While community after community has talked of comprehensive and integrated approaches to driving progress, Magnolia Place has met the challenge. Neighborhoods across the country should strive to achieve the same level of success for its residents.

Maximize Libraries

Libraries, neighborhoods, and local governments have unique opportunities to partner with one another in order to educate and empower the community and support their efforts.

A study by the Urban Libraries Council identified five main leadership roles of the public library: civic educator, conversation starter, community bridge, visionary and a center for democracy in action.

In its 2005 report, "The Engaged Library: Chicago Stories of Community Building," the council noted that libraries are ideal centralized locations for the collection of information, community networks, leaders, organizations, and local history. Through libraries these resources are made available to everyone and anyone and are especially useful to disengaged or new community members who are looking for more information on their surrounding community. Libraries, as centralized data centers, also make available general knowledge for those seeking to learn or develop new skills, or need further information pertaining to specific subjects.

In addition to a library's networking role, libraries further serve as places of civic education, where local residents have maximal access to community information. Local officials and librarians have often identified specific needs within their communities and then provide specified resources, training, and networking opportunities at the library. As the librarians identify community challenges, they can then create forums to discuss, share opinions, and propose ideas that can be used to develop action strategies. This is a unique role of public libraries because they are visible and action/knowledge oriented community organizations as well as central buildings within most communities.

NextDoor

Already in existence in over two thousand communities across the nation, NextDoor allows neighborhoods to create a customized social network—essentially a Facebook for every neighborhood. This system makes it safe to share online the kinds of things you would be okay sharing with your neighbors in person. Only those within the neighborhood network can see what is shared, and every neighbor has to verify his or her address. Since multiple neighborhoods make up a community, connecting with neighbors is an important first step in a successful community development initiative.

Blockboard

Blockboard is a mobile bulletin board that uses iPhone or Android phones to connect a neighborhood with the larger community. For instance, users can report graffiti, litter, or other problems to the city and automatically receive a follow-up status.

SkillShare

This is a community educational marketplace that lets all members learn or teach, especially families, educators, and students. Members use SkillShare's eBay-style website to exchange knowledge and information. Anyone can be a student or a teacher, or maybe both.

Programs like these will be critical to Latino communities in the future because Latinos so often operate in the informal economy. With access to this technology they can essentially use word of mouth to buy, sell, share, barter, or just cooperate to achieve common goals more easily and efficiently.

Healthy City

This is another established organization that brings community information and networks together in order to unite "community voices, rigorous research, and innovative technologies" that can address social inequalities within a community. The organization has created an online database that can be accessed and edited by anyone, at any time, and which also holds city research, data, demographics, organizations, and available services. Healthy City was designed to facilitate discussions and resource management among community leaders, with the goal of mutually beneficial collaboration among organizations, individuals, and data attainment initiatives. Specific services can also be located, per city, through the database search engine. In addition to locating services, the database can also create specified maps of the city reflecting general research, demographics, and services.

Neighborhood Program Opportunities

Zoning Flexibility

Though many Latino neighborhoods are thriving by any standard, others are not; in a sense, they are in catch-up mode. To accelerate their improvement and create momentum, a host of individual and group initiatives must take place. Because many of these projects would be run by individuals or small groups, flexibility is required so that time and expenses do not inhibit their undertaking or completion.

A forthcoming study, "Private and Public Responses to the 2011 Tornadoes," could shed light on how best to foster Latino neighborhood development. In an article in the *Wall Street Journal*, the authors of the study note that eight of ten affected businesses in tornado-ravaged Joplin, Missouri, have reopened, while less than half those in hard-hit Tuscaloosa, Alabama, have even applied for building permits. They note that Tuscaloosa chose a top-down approach guided by a redevelopment plan while Joplin took a bottom-up direction, allowing businesses to take the lead in recovery. Joplin's overall plan was brief and led by local businesses, while Tuscaloosa's was lengthy and authored by consultants.

Although everyone in Joplin is not entirely happy with this approach, it doesn't diminish its potential application in other communities.

The potential relevance to Latino neighborhoods seems clear. Relaxing some zoning regulations sends a message to residents and entrepreneurs that local investment is desired, individual and collective initiatives are welcome, and ultimately the neighborhood's future will be dictated by those who live in the area.

Some people might worry that this is a free-for-all, anything-goes approach—something that would be okay for barrios, maybe, but that would never be tolerated in upper-class neighborhoods. That is not the case. Certainly some planning is always a necessity; you do not want a liquor store next to a school or a factory next to a hospital, so most rules would continue to exist. But it is well known that bureaucracy and red tape are costly to small businesses, impeding their development or burdening them even before they open. The operational terms in this case are *flexibility* and *common sense*, but vigilance is key because Latino neighborhoods have historically been particularly burdened with polluting businesses.

A related issue is that of vacant lots—something traditionally stigmatized that can also be a community asset. It is becoming clear that even small pieces of open space can have a positive impact on urban dwellers. In some communities, "green vacant lots" have reportedly decreased gun assaults. As one official commented, "The neighborhoods where we've done a lot of this work are really transformed. The vacant lots host weddings and barbecues, instead of drug dealers and prostitutes" (Anonymous).

Neighborhoods of all types have found that urban gardening has huge benefits for children and adults and creates a sense of community and interaction in an easy and comfortable way. The resulting fruits, vegetables, and flowers offer both aesthetic and nutritional value.

Serve Neighborhood Consumers and Advance Wealth Creation

Families might have to leave their neighborhood to purchase some things, but not everything. There are plenty of opportunities for neighborhood entrepreneurs to provide products and services their neighbors want, from fresh fruits and vegetables to ethnic foods to children's toys (maybe used). On the service side there are win-win situations where those who do not work can support families with two out-of-home workers for a fee.

Additionally, the direct-selling sector, with $125 billion in global sales, offers full- and part-time opportunities through companies like Herbalife, Mary Kay, Primerica, The Pampered Chef, Avon, Shaklee, and hundreds of others.

NALCAB (National Association of Latino Community Asset-Builders)

Founded in 2002, NALCAB is a membership organization which represents more than seventy Latino-led community organizations from urban and rural communities throughout the United States. NALCAB's mission is to "build financial and human assets as well as real estate and technology resources in Latino families, communities, and organizations." The organization does this by networking, gathering Latino professionals (all experts in their respective fields), and taking charge of strategies for job creation and the building of neighborhood and family assets. More specifically, NALCAB has developed sustainable ways to bring technology to developing communities by involving and training local professionals to take charge of their own community initiatives.

Make Neighborhoods Safer

Prisoner reentry programs can benefit individuals, families, and neighborhoods. ComAlert (Community and Law Enforcement Resources Together) acts as a bridge between prison and community for parolees, offering job training, drug treatment, and counseling. Everyone benefits: the community, families, and the individual reentering the neighborhood.

Make Neighborhoods Healthier, Smarter, Baby-Friendlier

Nothing brings people together like a simple street fair or market. It gets people outdoors and gives neighbors a chance to mingle. Along with the entertainment, it also offers practical benefits. In some ways, farmers markets are the most beneficial choice, particularly when cost, selection, and quality meet and enable many neighborhoods to overcome their food desert situation. Obesity and related diseases like diabetes and hypertension are a threat not only to adults but also to children, and good nutrition is a major component in preventing chronic illnesses.

In a similar vein, baby fairs and education fairs have built-in audiences in most Latino neighborhoods. They offer a great opportunity for both residents and vendors, and they can facilitate public efforts to reach residents with information related to childhood vaccinations, preschool options, neighborhood safety, disaster preparedness, and much more.

Overall, ideas for neighborhood fairs are almost unlimited. They do not even have to be associated with a problem or issue—sometimes they can simply be fun. Often local residents have surprising artistic ability, making art fairs a perfect place to showcase their talents as well as an ideal get-acquainted opportunity. They also give communities a chance to recognize the capabilities of youth and build their self-esteem.

Supplement Smartphones

Many people in lower-income neighborhoods already maximize their smartphone capabilities, but in certain circumstances they need the power computers can offer. Free Wi-Fi at central locations can save residents time and money.

Let Others Do the Heavy Lifting

Neighborhoods are filled with busy people, so it makes sense to begin improving a community by taking advantage of services that already exist. Countless nonprofits, churches, governmental agencies, and even businesses spend heavily to reach residents with information about programs they offer, often free of charge. Yet participation rates in those programs are frequently very low. Neighborhoods should inventory these opportunities, and, through basic word of mouth, online communications, and standard marketing campaigns, make their neighbors aware of the help available to them.

There is so much that families and individuals can do to help one another and make the neighborhoods they share an asset rather than, in some cases, a liability. And while the residents of these areas are ultimately responsible for their advancement, there are countless people from areas far and wide that can lend help and support. That is the third strategy.

Advancing Support for Latino Neighborhood and Family Initiatives

It is possible to advance Latino families and youth in one generation. The United States is a nation that has embraced equal opportunity for natives and immigrants and their children over the course of its history. It is a nation that has benefited from the skills and work ethic of those with a burning desire to succeed. Latinos have already contributed to the nation—and they can do more. That is what this effort is all about. It will grow, family by family and neighborhood by neighborhood.

So how?

Build on a bold insight. UCLA professor David Hayes-Bautista understood decades ago that Latinos would be the young population that balanced an aging America.

Identify the core problem succinctly. There will be a growing gap in America between the number of available workers and the number needed to support an aging society. The younger populations, unfortunately, have a skills and education gap.

Frame the problem more fully. An overarching issue is that many Latinos immigrated after 1980 and missed the foundational years that would have eased their transition into the American workforce. Since then, issues of legal and "illegal" status have made Latino progress even more challenging. Latino families suffered when it became more difficult for Latino workers to move easily between Mexico and the United States in search of work. Language problems have slowed worker, family, and neighborhood progress. Due to lower incomes, Latinos have gravitated to poorer communities, resulting in attendance at lower-quality schools.

Follow a guiding premise.

1. As America ages it will need the young and growing Hispanic population, as well as others, to help reinvigorate the nation's work force and overall standard of living, help pay for the costs of an aging society, and support continued American competitiveness in the global economy.
2. Today the US Hispanic population is approximately 50 million, and it is projected to triple by 2050 when Hispanics, African Americans, and Asians will comprise an estimated 51 percent of the US population.
3. Though Latinos are hard-working, their current education and skill levels and the resulting estimated trajectory of their future progress leaves both them and the nation vulnerable.
4. Projected reductions in federal, state, and local budgets (regardless of who controls the White House and/or Congress) will require new approaches to accelerate overall Hispanic progress.
5. Despite the many challenges, Latinos must make significant progress in one generation in order to build momentum and ensure a strong future for themselves and the nation.

Allow a set of foundational principles to guide progress.

- By necessity, part with the old ideas, but keep the old values.
- Value context—understand the society in which Latinos are operating.

- Build on the modern, including technology, connectivity, and social networking.
- Let everyone own the effort, and empower young people from the very beginning.
- Manage the effort inside neighborhoods, but draw support from anyone willing to help.
- Appreciate both complex and simple solutions.
- Believe that your neighbors also have great ideas; embrace collective thinking.

Follow a goal and strategies designed to reach the goal

The Goal: Help Latino families prepare their children for mainstream success in one generation. This means helping them gain the necessary *knowledge and skills, understanding, and confidence, and a plan to build upon and advance.*

Strategies

To reach the overarching goal of helping Latino families prepare their children for mainstream success in one generation, there are three strategies:

- **First strategy:** Make households smarter.
- **Second strategy:** Strengthen neighborhoods and their support of the families within them.
- **Third strategy:** Advance integration of all sectors, including nonprofits, that support families and neighborhoods.

Implement at the Neighborhood Level Through Community-Based Organizations

Progress will ultimately come from work at the neighborhood level. It can come in many forms, large and small, so everyone can contribute. But for meaningful success, every neighborhood must have a plan. It can be complex, but a simple plan may initially be more effective and help bring more people into the process. Whatever the plan, in the beginning it will be the product of a few true believers, but others will follow. The development of even a rudimentary plan will send a positive signal to residents that the neighborhood cares and will invest in their future.

A plan will encourage nonprofits to increase focus on the area and possibly fill in gaps, like strengthening information flow on subjects important to families. Local officials may find ways to support the plan's initiatives. Businesses may notice that positive things are happening and that some small investments can both help the neighborhood and increase their visibility with local consumers. Foundations may notice funding opportunities, and former residents might see a chance to help others and the area they once called home. The possibilities are expansive.

For example, a simple plan might focus on neighborhood safety—Neighborhood Watch, perhaps, or a push for a traffic signal at a dangerous intersection, or street sweeping and graffiti cleanup. But what would really bring people together is greater interaction in the informal economy that was discussed earlier and that permeates every modest neighborhood. Improvements do not have to be complicated.

Social networking contributes to the informal economy. It builds connections among people who are striving to advance, allowing them to gain mutual support and knowledge in areas as diverse as finances, education, health, and even entertainment.

Local jurisdictions and public schools are continuously finding new ways to save money and still deliver important services. The ideas they draw on are sometimes simple, like cross-training public employees; rewarding high school students for graduating early; creating purchasing networks serving groups of schools or cities; and deputizing volunteers and seniors to help answer phones, direct traffic, and perform other basic services, with the savings supporting other, more complex public efforts.

Another critical strategy is coordinating the efforts of nonprofit groups. There has been a proliferation of 501(c)(3)s in community after community, and while the interest and desire to help is commendable, the result has been duplication, unnecessary competition, and donor confusion. This is a difficult issue to resolve, but it continues to raise concerns from a broad array of observers and participants at a time when coordination of efforts and maximization of every dollar is essential. While one model cannot be the answer for every community, the Magnolia Place effort described earlier in this book shows that coordination is possible and benefits many.

Conclusion

It is a competitive world, and the challenges it brings will only intensify as more people look to improve their lives. That is the main point of this book. Latinos can either close the gap with those who lead America—steadily raising their education and skills trajectory—or they can see their families fall further behind.

This book's approach to supporting families and neighborhoods is just that—an approach. It counts on parents, their neighbors, and even kids to make improvements in an almost ad-hoc manner because over time people have learned that planning societal change on a broad scale is almost impossible. In the Middle East, the Arab Spring took hold from the ground up—or was it from the Internet out?—taking hold in a million different directions. In a range of American cities, planners almost gave up on central city revitalization only to see pockets of energy pop up, often through the efforts of young people. The resulting momentum has changed the look of these areas.

In recognition of these changing dynamics, this book outlines the obliquity approach, which advances progress indirectly while acknowledging that families have great potential and, if supported, can move their families forward in powerful ways.

Some will ask whether this population is up to the task. I would ask, how can you doubt a group of people when some of them have walked hundreds of miles for minimum-wage job?

Notes

Introduction

The description of the years 1947–1973 (the formational years) reflect my personal remembrance of that time, and data that is evidence of the progress that so many Americans made.

The analysis of the decline of the American household income since 1973 came from the *New York Times* article "Innovation is Doing Little for Incomes," by Tyler Cowen, a professor at George Mason University, and was critical to much of my thinking.

Then There's the New Latino Timing

This chapter draws on the work of Manual Pastor, Vanessa Carter, and their associates at the Program for Environmental and Regional Equity (PERE) at the University of Southern California—work that has influenced much of my perspective on demographic changes in America. Even more important is their insight on the generational gap, which is still not on many radar screens despite its growing significance. Their research has been useful throughout this book.

The New Challenges Facing Latinos—and All Americans

Don Peck's illuminating article "Can the Middle Class Be Saved?" in the *Atlantic* succinctly outlines so many critical issues—from the steady changes in the US economy, to their impact on the middle class, to insights on who is winning and who is losing, to the plight of men who have done little to adapt to the changing world, and many more. Just as important are Peck's recommendations for policy changes, which give me hope that there are real actions we can take to change the course.

The Pew Center research highlighting minorities' increased optimism in some categories and youths' decreased belief in the nation's superiority is critically important for understanding how to work with Latino and other youth in these devastating times.

The research and analysis in Ronald Brownstein's thoughtful articles have always been valuable to me, contributing to my understanding of demographic and other societal changes.

In his *Los Angeles Times* article, "Low-wage work counts too," James Adler asks, "What jobs, for whom and at what cost?" These questions are important reminders that there are often in the understanding of problematic situations a range of trade-offs that must be evaluated.

Thomas A. Hemphill and Mark J. Perry's article in the *Wall Street Journal*, along with information from the *Economist*, helped me understand that while everyone wants more manufacturing in the United States, we are doing too little to ensure that we are generating the talent required for manufacturing jobs.

Robert Pastor's analysis of the significant trade opportunities with the US's neighbor nations to the north and south was another contribution to this book.

Economic Shifts Are Everywhere

In *The Great Stagnation*, Tyler Cowen discusses wage stagnation, the limited number of jobs from innovation, and particularly the primacy of private versus public good. I found his insights extremely useful as I thought about the economic future of the US and Latinos.

The problem of lagging skills, powerfully highlighted in *Race Against the Machine*, suggests that incremental educational improvements won't be enough to advance most people.

The Great Disruption, which outlines most people's worsening economic situation, serves as fair warning, reinforcing for me the need for Latinos and others to recognize the importance of support networks as they try to build a solid future in this challenging era.

I appreciate the wisdom in *The Power of Pull (Hagel III, Brown, Davison)*. It is not enough to gain education and skills; to succeed in this new economy, it will be critical to understand how the world works, especially how the fast flow of information and global changes impact all areas.

Adam Davidson from *Planet Money* and Michael Spence in *Foreign Affairs* both helped me to understand that all quality jobs are not equal. There are ranges of compensation within job categories and differences between domestic and foreign products, or tradable goods.

Finally, *The Coming Jobs War* helps set the context for understanding a wide range of issues, from trade and emerging markets to attitudes about work and the priorities of the average person in different parts of the world.

A Perspective on the Future

An early and influential book that used demographics to help predict the future is *The Burden of Support: Young Latinos in an Aging Society*, by David E. Hayes-Bautista, Werner O. Schink, and Jorge Chapa.

The Post-American World by Fareed Zakaria helped me put the broader world in perspective because it made the important point that while America's relative decline is debatable, the fact that many nations in the merging world are "upping their game" is undeniable. From my perspective, this growing challenge to the United States makes investment in all its people essential.

Thinking and Finding Answers

Even though this section of the book is relatively brief, in my view it is critically important. While I have always been curious, I was also very fortunate to be able to "think about thinking," particularly in my career at Humana, Inc. I pursued unique interests, but mainly I learned from the many people I worked with who also pursued new ideas and worked hard to find better ways to do things.

Bob Johansen and his ideas in *Get There Early* also influenced this chapter.

While I've been influenced by many great thinkers, I was particularly drawn to the insights in *Smart World* by Richard Ogle. For me, the key takeaways have to do with crossing boundaries, understanding the space of ideas, and breakthrough thinking. I focused on his notion that "what we need exists" and that ability to link ideas is a critical challenge and opportunity.

This section was certainly influenced by the book *Nudge* and a range of other ideas from the business sector. This makes sense to me because, as I have argued for some time, all organizations share some things in common. The research in the area of decision fatigue is very important, in part because it makes those fortunate enough to have resources recognize that while they might empathize, they do not fully understand the obstacles that the poor battle every day. Cornell University's work on improving cafeterias so students eat better is an important reminder that solutions do not have to be complex and expensive—just well thought out.

How Do Latinos See Themselves?

First, Oscar Arias sets a high bar for candor, which we might all learn from, and so does Jorge Castaneda, former foreign minister of Mexico and currently professor at New York University, whose recent book is *Manna Forever*. John Meyers demonstrates in his article, "From Farmingville to East Hampton," that direct appraisals of situations are possible and helpful. Ultimately this was my call, having watched, lived, and been part of the Latino culture my whole life.

I do think that, increasingly, Latinos need to evaluate themselves within the context of the one-generation goal. I see no other option.

The Future That's Already Happened

Virginia Postrel's book was influential to my view that we have to challenge the future, and *Obliquity* provided powerful insight about how to do it. What more can you ask for?

Moving Forward

The insights on the changing immigration situation, which are so critical to this book, came from an article by Jorge Castaneda and Douglas S. Massey and the work of Dowell Meyers, a professor at the University of Southern California.

I would like to attribute the nine reasons for business failure, but I cannot find the resource. I apologize.

Making Households Smarter

Once again, *Obliquity* drives much of this section. I've also been fortunate to be around people who understand and appreciate analysis, thinking, and strategy, and their influence is apparent in these pages.

Daniel Gross's article reaffirms the important notion that everything should be open to questioning—in this case the value of "ownership"—but the lists includes many other areas, particularly if we want to advance important change.

My thanks to the following programs and organizations for the work they do:

- Centro Latino for Literacy
- Reading Eggs
- iMentor

- Project K-Nect
- Crear Futuros
- Gamification
- Scratch
- AT&T Mobile Apps
- Apple in Education
- MyMoney.gov
- Jump$tart
- College Match

Strengthening Latino Neighborhoods

My neighborhood strategy builds on the powerful concept of social networking. In fact, I believe we should think of neighborhoods not as a collection of buildings, but as a social network of people who can directly influence each other's lives. The power of collective thinking as described in *Crowdsourcing* and *The Wisdom of Crowds* is also fundamental to this neighborhood strategy.

I appreciate the input I received from those at Magnolia Place in Los Angeles, but I value their daily work even more. They are a national model for neighborhoods throughout the nation.

Again, I'd like to acknowledge the programs listed below:

- NextDoor
- Blockboard
- SkillShare
- Healthy City

About the Author

Steve Moya

In an increasingly complex world, those with broad and varied backgrounds are best suited to find bolder solutions for organizations and people. By always challenging the status quo and connecting ideas from different fields, Steve Moya has been able to guide groups to new and better outcomes. His experience and knowledge comes from a background that includes the corporate, entrepreneurial, public, and consulting fields, and companies and entities that include Univision; the Los Angeles City Council; Moya, Villanueva and Associates; and Humana Inc.

Born in East Los Angeles into a family that immigrated to the United States in the late 1920s, he has firsthand knowledge of the challenges that Latinos and other populations face in their efforts to advance. He has supported the community through involvement with Latino organizations in areas as diverse as political empowerment, literacy, policy research, the arts, and many educational initiatives.

What distinguishes Moya's writing is his critical thinking, which builds from his expertise in change management, strategy development, trend analysis, communications, marketing, and situational analysis and planning. His view is that the world is becoming more competitive, and those that advance (whether people or companies) cannot simply do things slightly better—they must find new ways to meet the demands of the marketplace and society. While this may be easier for organizations, all individuals can work at this and improve their lives. Take the use of social networks: in low-income neighborhoods, people can connect either electronically or personally with neighbors to tap expertise, share resources, exchange services, and build skills to fill the gaps in their lives and create opportunities for their children.

Acknowledgements

Over the years I've been curious about changes in the "world" and have been fortunate to be able to apply that knowledge with a range of companies selling products, service and ideas. At one point I began to ask myself what these changes meant to the broad Latino community and my conclusion was more than we know. So I wrote an article on the subject and share it with Antonia Hernandez who had moved to the California Community Foundation from MALDEF. She said I needed to write a book. I disagreed, and here's the book. She not only drove the book, but offered input, resources and staff support. I thank her and her staff.

Jesus Rangel liked the book idea and supported it in many ways, but was always focused on using the book to make positive change in Latino communities across the country. Carlos Santiago and Omar Guttierez of Santiago Solutions Group helped with research and the charts included in the book and offered input along the way. Dr. Leo Estrada at UCLA contributed critical insights that strengthened the books direction and I am appreciative of his thinking.

Alexandra Seros and Jan Phares helped at pivotal points with help that made everything easier.

David E. Hayes-Bautista, Werner O. Schink and Jorge Chapa's book **The Burden of Support: Young Latinos in an Aging Society** set much of my thinking in motion years ago. They were visionaries.

My wife Rita has always been there with support for this and other projects and offered great ideas as well. I can't thank her enough. Finally I'd like thank my father, Oscar Moya for keeping interesting discussion alive in our family for as long as I can remember.

www.ingramcontent.com/pod-product-compliance
Lightning Source LLC
Chambersburg PA
CBHW020535290526
45786CB00002B/881